Praise for the series

It was only a matter of time before a clever publisher realized that there is an audience for whom *Exile on Main Street* or *Electric Ladyland* are as significant and worthy of study as *The Catcher in the Rye* or *Middlemarch* . . . The series . . . is freewheeling and eclectic, ranging from minute rock-geek analysis to idiosyncratic personal celebration
—*The New York Times Book Review*

Ideal for the rock geek who thinks liner notes just aren't enough
—*Rolling Stone*

One of the coolest publishing imprints on the planet
—*Bookslut*

These are for the insane collectors out there who appreciate fantastic design, well-executed thinking, and things that make your house look cool. Each volume in this series takes a seminal album and breaks it down in startling minutiae. We love these. We are huge nerds
—*Vice*

A brilliant series . . . each one a work of real love
—*NME* (UK)

Passionate, obsessive, and smart
—*Nylon*

Religious tracts for the rock 'n' roll faithful

[A] cor

T0204967

We . . . aren't naive enough to think that we're your only source for reading about music (but if we had our way . . . watch out). For those of you who really like to know everything there is to know about an album, you'd do well to check out Bloomsbury's "33 1/3" series of books
—*Pitchfork*

For almost twenty years, the 33 1/3 series of music books has focused on individual albums by acts well known (Bob Dylan, Nirvana, Abba, Radiohead), cultish (Neutral Milk Hotel, Throbbing Gristle, Wire) and many levels in-between. The range of music and their creators defines "eclectic," while the writing veers from freewheeling to acutely insightful. In essence, the books are for the music fan who (as Rolling Stone noted) "thinks liner notes just aren't enough."
—*The Irish Times*

For reviews of individual titles in the series, please visit our blog at 333sound.com and our website at http://www.bloomsbury.com/musicandsoundstudies

Follow us on Twitter: @333books

Like us on Facebook: https://www.facebook.com/33.3books

For a complete list of books in this series, see the back of this book.

Forthcoming in the series:

Blackout

Natasha Lasky

BLOOMSBURY ACADEMIC
NEW YORK • LONDON • OXFORD • NEW DELHI • SYDNEY

BLOOMSBURY ACADEMIC
Bloomsbury Publishing Inc
1385 Broadway, New York, NY 10018, USA
50 Bedford Square, London, WC1B 3DP, UK
29 Earlsfort Terrace, Dublin 2, Ireland

BLOOMSBURY, BLOOMSBURY ACADEMIC and the Diana logo are trademarks of
Bloomsbury Publishing Plc

First published in the United States of America 2023

Copyright © Natasha Lasky, 2023

For legal purposes the Acknowledgments on p. viii constitute an extension
of this copyright page.

All rights reserved. No part of this publication may be reproduced or transmitted
in any form or by any means, electronic or mechanical, including photocopying,
recording, or any information storage or retrieval system, without prior permission
in writing from the publishers.

Bloomsbury Publishing Inc does not have any control over, or responsibility for, any
third-party websites referred to or in this book. All internet addresses given in
this book were correct at the time of going to press. The author and publisher
regret any inconvenience caused if addresses have changed or sites have
ceased to exist, but can accept no responsibility for any such changes.

Whilst every effort has been made to locate copyright holders the publishers would be
grateful to hear from any person(s) not here acknowledged.

Library of Congress Cataloging-in-Publication Data
Names: Lasky, Natasha, author.
Title: Britney Spears's Blackout / Natasha Lasky. Description: [1st.] |
New York : Bloomsbury Academic, 2021. | Series: 33 1/3 |
Summary: "Discusses Blackout as a transitional album and a crucial
hinge between twentieth and twenty-first-century pop"– Provided by publisher.
Identifiers: LCCN 2022008921 (print) | LCCN 2022008922 (ebook) |
ISBN 9781501377594 (paperback) | ISBN 9781501377600 (epub) |
ISBN 9781501377617 (pdf) | ISBN 9781501377624
Subjects: LCSH: Spears, Britney. Blackout. | Spears, Britney–Criticism and interpretation. |
Popular music–1991–2000–History and criticism. |
Popular music–2001–2010–History and criticism. Classification:
LCC ML420.S714 L37 2021 (print) | LCC ML420.S714 (ebook) |
DDC 782.42164092–dc23
LC record available at https://lccn.loc.gov/2022008921
LC ebook record available at https://lccn.loc.gov/2022008922

ISBN: PB: 978-1-5013-7759-4
ePDF: 978-1-5013-7761-7
eBook: 978-1-5013-7760-0

Series: 33 1/3

Typeset by Newgen KnowledgeWorks Pvt. Ltd., Chennai, India
Printed and bound in the United States of America

To find out more about our authors and books visit www.bloomsbury.com
and sign up for our newsletters.

Contents

Acknowledgments

Blackout is a testament to the power of thoughtful collaboration. Though I hesitate to compare this book to one of the greatest pop albums of the twenty-first century, I want to follow *Blackout*'s lead and foreground the contributions of those who made this book possible.

Thank you to the 33 1/3 team at Bloomsbury Academic for giving me the opportunity to write this book in the first place.

I appreciate Luis, Gabriel, and Jordan Miller for their participation in the book, their generosity, and their invaluable insights into the Britney fan community.

Thank you to Jeff Weiss, Sasha Geffen, and John Seabrook for offering me their advice about taking on a project like this and their expertise about Britney.

I owe deep gratitude to my friends and roommates who have supported me throughout the process and tolerated me talking their ears off about the latest Britney news: Anand Bradley, Claire Dickson, Olivia Oldham, Eli Zuzovsky, Emily Shen, Liv Weinstein, L. G. Fadiman, Freddie Shanel, Lincoln Sorscher, Isabel Levin, Saul Glist, Eli Holmes, and Frank Cahill.

Ruby Drake, Sebastian Kleppe, Max Sokoloff, Clio Gevirtz, Soraya Okuda, Isaiah Dufort, Charlie Blecker, and Rachel Clyde are brilliant editors who strengthened the bones of the book—I still thought about their notes months after they gave them.

Julia Fine, Cat Zhang, Isa Flores-Jones, Carl Denton, and Paul Sullivan gave thoughtful feedback just in the nick of time. Their work is a natural extension of their friendship—their honesty and careful consideration made editing feel like a form of care. The way they unite kindness and intellectual rigor has guided me both in the writing of this book and beyond.

Thanks to Jameson Johnson for her invaluable friendship. Being around her curiosity, sense of humor, and adventurous spirit made this book possible.

I'm so grateful for Jonathan Sandoval, who has inspired me with his gentleness and openness to the world. He nurtured the vulnerable parts of myself that allow me to write.

Lily Scherlis has been reading drafts of this book since the proposal stage and has been editing my work for as long as I've been writing. She has pushed my ideas and prose further than I ever thought they could go. I owe so much of who I am and how I write to her friendship.

I would have never written this book were it not for Spencer Glesby: they introduced me to *Blackout* and encouraged me to apply to 33 1/3. They move me with their thoughtfulness, intelligence, sense of humor, passion for music, and encyclopedic knowledge of pop culture. If I've emulated even a fraction of their wisdom over the course of this book, I've succeeded.

Thank you to Cecilia for her genuine belief in the book and in me as a writer. Her enthusiasm and curiosity buoyed me throughout the process—I will always treasure the road trip where we listened to *Blackout* together. I am so grateful to Anna, Ben, Mitch, and Lucia. They've taught me more about music than anyone.

If I were to list all the ways Elliot Schiff has supported me and the writing of this book, the acknowledgments would be longer than the book itself. He fact checked and proofread and galvanized me at my lowest moments and reminded me of the worth of my ideas. He has allowed me to put my mind and heart into this book, fully. I can't thank him enough.

Introduction

In November 2004, for perhaps the first time in her adult life, Britney Spears had some free time. At twenty-two, she had been working nonstop for almost a decade. She started as a pip-squeak belting her heart out on *The Mickey Mouse Club*, and at sixteen, released her first single, the slinky, iconic ". . . Baby One More Time." For the song's music video, she pitched a scene (she's stuck in a classroom thinking about boys) and a costume (a modified school uniform with a short skirt and a crop top). The moment she tapped her platform shoe against her chair in the video's opening shots, Britney established the aesthetic that would come to define her pop persona, one that toed the line between starry-eyed innocence and hip-swaying lust. This vision paid off. ". . .Baby One More Time" sold ten million copies by the time she was eighteen. Her 1999 debut album of the same name went platinum within a month of its release. Between 2000 and 2003, she released three more albums: *Oops!... I Did It Again*, *Britney*, and *In the Zone*, all of which debuted at the top of the charts. If you were alive in the early aughts, I'd bet that you could conjure her most iconic looks—the red latex bodysuit in the music video for *Oops!... I Did It Again*, the anaconda draped around her shoulders in her 2001 VMA performance of "I'm A Slave 4 U"—even if you never listened to a single one of her albums.

But after a near-constant stream of record rollouts, tours, movie roles, music videos, press conferences, and VMA appearances, Britney was sick of pop stardom. "I've actually learned to say 'NO!'" she wrote on her blog in late 2004. "With this newly found freedom, it's like people don't know how to act around me." She could continue to make music, but she could also quit forever, move home, and start a family with her husband, Kevin Federline. "I don't think I'll do another tour for a couple of years," she wrote, "My priorities in life have changed. I am having fun again reading all the magazines that I enjoy (mainly because I am not on them). At this point and time, what I want is not my face on every cover, but someone else's instead."[1]

When rumors arose that Britney had given up music for good, she reassured her fans that she'd return to the studio eventually. But she wanted things to change. Throughout her career, in interviews and on red carpets, she seemed the consummate girl-next-door, soft-spoken and polite, often ending her sentences with a flash of her signature toothy smile and a hearty giggle. But this demureness masked her intensity and ambition. Over the five years following her debut single, she developed a reputation for being a hard worker, a team player, and an impeccable performer. On stage, Britney hit even her smallest marks—a hip flick, a shoulder shake—with absolute precision, and she'd do it over and over again. Even though she had less experience in the studio, she observed and asked questions until she could begin to write songs herself. She was, by most of her collaborators' accounts, a firebrand: opinionated and clearheaded in her vision.

She was also, when she got started, a teenage girl. No matter how many smart decisions she made or clever lyrics she wrote or jaw-dropping dance moves she executed, her label, Jive Records, was not keen on letting her steer her career. Her contract, signed only a few years after she was voted "Junior High Most Beautiful," likely put her at a disadvantage. We don't know what's in it, but the music industry, and Jive Records in particular, isn't exactly known for its fair contracts, especially not in the late 1990s. Jive had a precedent for signing teens under exploitative conditions. Besides, fame can be so tenuous. Britney's fifteen minutes could have ended just as abruptly as it began. She didn't want to rock the boat. So when someone told her to do something, for the most part, she didn't just do it—she did it perfectly.

Her preternatural ability to satisfy the demands of her team and audience alike meant that at her early-2000's peak, Britney had created a persona that could take any form and still move records. She was a girl-next-door and an untouchable siren, a bubbly teen and a sophisticated career woman, a bimbo corrupting the children and a good Christian girl, a white-trash reality TV star and elegant red-carpet royalty, a spineless corporate tool and a visionary calling the shots. She cultivated intimacy and distance simultaneously. She dropped enough hints about her inner life to string us along, but never let us get too close. Her blank-slate quality, peppered with her star power, made her ubiquitous; she could become anyone her audience wanted her to be—and still be unmistakably Britney. But at twenty-three, Britney, newly married, fresh off a fifty-four-show tour, could become someone new. After so many years of molding herself to please an audience, her adulthood unspooled before her, full of possibility.

Though Britney wanted to take a break from music, she occasionally speculated about her next steps. She hoped to write more of her own material, like she did on 2003's *In the Zone*, her fourth and then most recent album. On *In the Zone*, Britney explored her own point of view in her music, writing on nine out of the album's thirteen songs. One of these, "Everytime," was a creative breakthrough. With soft piano and plaintive, earnest lyrics, Britney expresses her pain with a direct, stripped-down singer-songwriter aesthetic anathema to the upbeat pop anthems that made her famous. She also wrote a series of tracks for *In the Zone*—"Look Who's Talking Now," "It Feels Nice" (also known as "Sin City,") and "Rockstar"—all of which rage against the people that wronged her, from opportunistic ex Justin Timberlake to the bigwig execs at her label. "This business is fucked," she raps on "Sin City," displaying a world-weariness that we had never heard from her before. But her label cut these songs from the final track list. In a Japanese press conference for *In the Zone*, she hinted at her frustration with her team butting into her music: "I really know how the process works now, and I know I can do it on my own."[2]

After a period of radio silence, we got our first taste of this new, more independent Britney in December 2004, just a few weeks after she announced she was taking a break. At KIIS FM, a radio station in Burbank, DJ Jesse Lozano was on the air when an assistant told him: "Britney Spears is on the phone. She says she wants to play her new song."

An hour later, Britney showed up at the studio barefoot, ambling across the parking lot with her chihuahua and a bodyguard, clutching a CD. The paparazzi usually trailed her wherever she went, but here, there wasn't a camera in sight. She handed him the CD with her latest single and he took it to the studio. She called the song "Mona Lisa."

"Mona Lisa" hinted at a new era for Britney, one where, on and off the mic, she spoke for herself. In the song, Britney tells a dark fairy tale about the cruelty of the spotlight. The lyrics describe a woman, "Mona Lisa," that "everyone knows so well," but she suffers behind the scenes, fearing a scandal-hungry public who just "wants her to break down." The song's title, a wink to fans in the know, references a pseudonym Britney had been using for years. When she directed her first music video, for her 2004 single "Do Somethin'," she credited herself as "Mona Lisa." She told MTV show Total Request Live: "I kinda think she's like my alter ego. Whenever I feel like being mean or possibly like bustin' people around to get stuff right, it's kinda easier to be called 'Mona Lisa' instead of Britney." The pseudonym articulated her rage, disappointment, and ennui, emotions that, especially for a pop star in 2004, couldn't easily be wrapped in cellophane and sold.

By naming "Mona Lisa" after an alter ego, the song seems like a frank admission that in the past, she felt that she could only express truth through fiction. All signs—her blog, her demo, even her impromptu arrival to the radio station, chihuahua in tow—pointed to a Britney who wanted to call the shots and release her music on her own terms, no matter how her label felt about it. On "Mona Lisa's" radio debut, Britney even mentioned that she had a new album in the works. It was halfway done, she assured, and it already had a name: *Original Doll.*

It turned out that the album was in rougher shape than Britney had insinuated. A representative for Jive told *Billboard* that "Mona Lisa" was not getting a traditional release, and that "no album is scheduled at the moment." Still, "Mona Lisa" was evidence of Britney's maturing perspective and her willingness to expose more vulnerable, unvarnished parts of her persona. A second song recorded during the *Original Doll* sessions, "Someday (I Will Understand)," depicts a Britney in touch with her sadness, fed up with fame, and looking for deeper meaning. Her signature innocent-yet-knowing sensuality is nowhere to be found on her tracks for *Original Doll.* On "Mona Lisa," she sounds cutting and jaded, and on "Someday" quietly reflective—subtler emotions than love, sex, and heartbreak, the typical bombastic feelings that populate Top 40 pop, and much of Britney's previous work.

But just as Britney prepared to speak her truth for the first time, her private life got thrust into the spotlight. Work on *Original Doll* stagnated and, as the years passed, scandals trickled in one after the other. She had two sons with K-Fed, and filed for divorce a couple of years later. From 2006 to 2008, the tabloid headlines became a laundry list of her mistakes: driving with her son on her lap, dropping her newborn, exposing her crotch, checking in and out of rehab, getting charged with six months in jail for a hit-and-run, losing custody of her kids. The paparazzi pursued her so doggedly that she often lashed out, cussing at them and even attacking them physically. It felt like Britney was hemorrhaging the public's good will, growing unrecognizable even to her fans.

Her teen-pop image finally imploded in 2007, when she now infamously shaved her head on a whim while getting extensions in the suburbs outside Los Angeles. Her hairdresser pressed in tufts of blond hair one by one until Britney swatted her hand away and said "I just don't want anybody, anybody touching my head. I don't want anyone touching my hair. I'm sick of people touching me."[3] She grabbed an electric razor and shaved her head. The image of Britney, wandering through a parking lot in the dead of night, bald-headed, washed out by the flash of a digital camera, couldn't be further from the iconic images of Britney at her most blonde and nubile. While her previous scandals could be blamed on the paparazzi, this incident seemed to be her fault—*she* had chosen to make herself "ugly." The poised Princess of Pop was nowhere to be seen. Instead, she seemed unhinged enough to destroy her carefully cultivated beauty in a single night. In early 2007, the public could finally pin her down. She was neither a seductress nor a girl next door: she was a trainwreck.

But there was still some hope that Britney would revive her image. At the height of her breakdown, *MTV News* published a list of dos and don'ts for the erstwhile starlet, ostensibly to help guide her back into the public's good graces, but more likely an excuse to make fun of her. Don't: hang out with Paris Hilton; chew gum or smoke in public; wear knotty extensions; one-up your ex, Kevin Federline. Do: stay away from Vegas; wear designer clothes; hang out with friends from back home in Kentwood; update your website; get a publicist.[4] Perhaps most cutting, they told her to take a cue from her rival, Christina Aguilera. Even when Aguilera dabbled in oiled-up sex appeal in her album *Dirrrty*, she remained "classy" and consistent, releasing new music at a steady clip. Britney could reclaim the throne if she began to churn out the pop hits she was known for, just like in the old days—MTV suggested she reach out to the hot producers of the moment, Timbaland and Pharrell, or even her old mainstay Max Martin. She had a shot at a comeback, she just had to write the music to accompany it.

Even though *Original Doll* had been scrapped, it turned out that a comeback album was already in the works. Britney managed to record it throughout 2006 and 2007, between jaunts to celebrity haunts like Guy's Bar and Les Deux. On her blog, Britney posted a list of potential titles for this newest release. The options seemed to suggest that she was in a better place, between self-help cliches like "Dignity" and "Integrity," sexy taunts like "Down Boy," and lighthearted but incoherent fragments like "Omg Is Lindsay Lohan Like Ok Like." Veering between playfulness and positivity, these titles suggested that perhaps Britney would respond to the public scrutiny with some heartfelt piano ballads like her 2003 hit "Everytime," in which she reveals her previous battles with loneliness and depression in thin, fragile vocals. After all, this is the playbook for pop: make a mistake, and then respond with the sonic hallmarks of authenticity—acoustic guitars, clean vocals, vague yet sufficiently plaintive lyrics.

When Jive rolled out the album in fall of 2007, it wasn't what anyone expected. She didn't pick any of the titles she brainstormed on her blog. Instead, she called the album *Blackout*, as if she'd recorded it during a bender, stumbling into the booth in a drunken stupor. The cover presents Britney at her least recognizable, her signature blond locks hidden behind a black wig. The album, running a tight forty-three minutes, begins with "It's Britney, Bitch" and then explodes into screeds about the pressures of fame in "Gimme More" and "Piece of Me." Then, the record launches into a series of bouncy club bangers, from the breathy "Break the Ice" to the thumping, lush "Get Naked (I Got a Plan)" and the wobbly, bass-heavy "Freakshow." *Blackout's* momentum doesn't let up until the Neptunes-penned breakup anthem "Why Should I Be Sad" ends the album on a contemplative note, like the sun peering over the horizon after a long night out. Unlike *In the Zone*, *Blackout* has no tearful ballads; the album is packed to the brim with high-BPM, four-on-the-floor beats, heavily distorted vocals, and booming bass. There doesn't seem to be any non-digital instruments on the record, and even Britney's vocals are manipulated nearly beyond recognition. There are no features on the album, yet mysterious voices—cackles, whispers, echoes—crowd Britney's on nearly every song. Synths swirl, pitches drop. You never know what sound is coming next.

Blackout seemed dead on arrival; as the only album in her discography that didn't debut at number one, *Blackout* was the worst-performing album of her career thus far. Only one of its singles, "Gimme More," cracked *Billboard's* top ten. Most critics, even those that liked *Blackout*, dismissed

Britney as a vacant has-been, one breakdown away from ending her career. Even her most carefully honed talent, dancing, seemed out of her reach. In September of 2007, she performed "Gimme More" at the VMAs, listlessly shuffling with a blank expression, barely able to lip-sync along to her own song. A few months after the performance, the Associated Press prepared her obituary, just in case.

The album confirmed her detractors' worst vision of her. On *Blackout*, Britney didn't seem like the ditzy cheerleader she played in her teen-pop days—she seemed like a mess, singing about her many nights of drinking, fucking, and dancing. Her producers distorted and pitch-corrected her voice until she sounded like a robot, seeming to uphold the rumor that she couldn't sing without digital alteration. If Britney was so fed up with tabloid rumors—that she was a bad mom, a sex addict, a drug-addled party girl—why would she inhabit that persona so confidently on *Blackout*?

Critics emphasized that Britney was a mess behind the scenes of *Blackout* as well, suspecting that she was too mired in her own dramas to meaningfully contribute to the album. Though she was *Blackout*'s executive producer—a title she held for the only time in her career—critics didn't know how much agency this title afforded her. She is credited on only two songs on *Blackout*, "Freakshow" and "Ooh Ooh Baby." There are accounts of her scribbling lyrics on a Starbucks napkin, but it's unclear whether the songs she wrote were cut from the album, or whether her contributions simply went uncredited. From interviews with her producers and A&R, it seems that she had a more curatorial role on *Blackout*, helping select producers and set the overall tone of the album while others, for the most part, wrote the songs. During the recording of *Blackout*, Britney was suffering from postpartum depression, battling with her ex-husband for custody over her children and scuffling with the paparazzi, so she couldn't spend as much time in the studio as she would have liked.

In any case, she didn't promote *Blackout*, save for a single radio interview with Ryan Seacrest, during which her manager, Sam Lutfi, and her assistant woke her up from a nap and put her on speaker. The interview is a far cry from her previous tightly-curated album rollouts. There are murmurs the microphone doesn't pick up; Seacrest often can't hear Britney's answers to his relatively banal questions. Seacrest asks Britney if she'd do anything to celebrate the album's release, and she laughs.

***

After 2007, Britney seemed to recover. Over time, both the narrative surrounding *Blackout* and Britney's career have been rewritten, and Britney has transformed into a totally different kind of celebrity. In November 2008, she gave her critics the comeback record they wanted, *Circus*. The album is standard Britney fare: bouncy, danceable tracks that speak to her free-spirit sexuality and love of performance. *Circus* spent nine weeks in the top ten, and became her most successful record on the charts at the time, save for *Oops!... I Did It Again* and "...Baby One More Time." While Britney didn't take *Blackout* on the road, *Circus* got a world tour. Some saw the *Circus* tour as a trojan horse for *Blackout*, as the setlist featured more tracks from *Blackout* than from its namesake. Still, *Circus* gave the tour its purpose, theme, and name. She sang *Blackout*'s songs about the horrors of life in the public eye from the safe vantage of seeming-recovery.

In February 2008, Britney's father filed for a conservatorship over Britney and got it. The conservatorship gave all control over her mental health, finances, and career decisions to her father and a lawyer ominously named Andrew Wallet. This restrictive arrangement raised a few red flags for her fans, but at the time the mainstream media thought it was a good decision to let her family steer the ship. Besides, Britney appeared to be her old self again, or at least a facsimile of it, singing about how much she loved the spotlight. All the darkness she hinted at in "Mona Lisa" and *Blackout* seemed to disappear. Never mind the Britney in 2004, writing on her blog, freshly married, who could do anything, even quit music altogether. That Britney never seemed further away. She no longer had a choice; Britney was back in the spotlight—this time, for good.

She continued to put out music, and performed 248 times at her blockbuster Vegas residency, starting in 2013, over the course of four years. Other than her residency, Britney remained, for the most part, out of the public eye, save for her Instagram posts, in which she twirled in low-rise shorts, painted, and detailed her daily follies (like the time she left a lit candle in her home gym and accidentally burned it down).

Over the course of Britney's conservatorship, our relationship with celebrity culture changed. In 2010, strengthened anti-paparazzi laws prevented photographers from stalking other A-listers the way they had stalked Britney. With social media, we didn't need the tabloids anymore. If we wanted to see pictures of our favorite celebrities going about their lives, we didn't have to refresh *TMZ* or flip through

US Weekly—we could just check Instagram. It had become more difficult for the mainstream media to gang up on a star like they did Britney. Social media amplified the voices of Britney's fans, the Britney Army, who organized to defend her against bad press and go after her detractors.

Similarly, time has looked fondly on *Blackout*. Upon release, critics were divided on the album, but in retrospect, negative critics' interpretations of *Blackout* as the superficial ramblings of a woman trapped in a never-ending bender, too wasted or distraught to sing without auto-tune, rang false. The Britney on *Blackout* is jaded and sharp-tongued. She sees herself not as an anomaly, or a tragic figure, but as a victim of a predatory industry that'll turn a woman's breakdown into a goldmine. She may not like the constant surveillance—who would?—but there's not a lot she can do about it. She's just one woman. In this context, her promiscuous, club-hopping persona on *Blackout* is a form of resistance. She may not be able to escape the tabloids, but she can still have a good time.

This interpretation of *Blackout* as a narrative of redemption and resilience has come to define Britney's career: "It's Britney, Bitch" became her catchphrase, and her Vegas residency and ensuing tour were both called "Piece of Me" after one of *Blackout's* singles. In the 2010s, *Rolling Stone* championed the album. Pop critic Rob Sheffield published a piece about Lady Gaga's hit "Telephone," which Gaga had originally written for Britney. He attributed the success of "Telephone," and the broader rise of electro-pop in the 2010s, in part to Britney's influence. "'Telephone' actually sounds a lot like Britney's 2007 hit 'Piece of Me', proving yet again how much impact Britney has had on the sonics of current pop," he wrote. "People love to make fun of Britney, and why not, but if 'Telephone' proves anything, it's that *Blackout* may be the most influential pop album of the past five years."[5] In 2012, *Blackout* was inducted into the Rock n' Roll Hall of Fame, and the record made *Rolling Stone's* 2020 list of the 500 greatest albums of all time.

For people who didn't like the record, its digital qualities felt at best, alienating and ugly, and at worst, compensatory for Britney's weak singing voice. Over time, they were reconsidered as forward-looking. The EDM-inflected pop on *Blackout*, a rarity on the charts when it came out, went on to dominate the Top 40 throughout the 2010s, from Ke$ha's trashy electro-pop to Skrillex's warped dubstep. *Blackout's* influence has even crept into the avant-garde. PC Music, a small British label, developed an experimental form of pop whose signature sonic qualities, like chipmunk pitched-up vocals and clanging metallic synths, were amplified, uncanny versions of *Blackout's* sound. *Blackout* stopped being the dying gasp of a woman in peril and became the soundtrack of the future.

Seeing *Blackout's* story as an arc from thwarted comeback record to genre-defying classic is narratively satisfying. But *Blackout* still resists categorization. The album teems with contradictions. The record's dark, chaotic sound reflected the turmoil of Britney's personal life in a way that none of her albums would ever again, but it's not a strictly confessional album like the shelved *Original Doll*, either—in an ironic twist, *Blackout* presents itself as Britney's reclamation of her narrative, but credits her on only two songs. *Blackout* didn't engineer her comeback in any traditional sense, but it formed a turning point in Britney's career, transforming her from the effortlessly perky teen queen into a nightmare: campy, fatalistic, and weird.

The things that make *Blackout* great—its ambiguity, its collaborative spirit, its bitter wit, its strangeness, its tightrope walk between euphoria and terror—allow Britney to be evasive, confusing, and inconsistent, a person rather than a persona. In some ways, *Blackout* fulfilled, and even exceeded, the subversive aims of *Original Doll*. There is no "real Britney" on *Blackout* that can be packaged up and sold; the album encourages a more complex narrative.

This book will tell the story of the album's production and reception following *Blackout*'s interpretive lead, incorporating Britney's contradictions rather than sweeping them under the rug. In doing so, we can see *Blackout* not just as an album but a space of possibility. *Blackout*, with its lush, dark, disorienting sound, evokes the grimy Hollywood clubs Britney frequented while she recorded the album. In the darkness of the club, the particularities of a person disappear—everyone becomes a silhouette, even Britney Spears.

Notes

1   Spears, Britney. "Letters of Truth." *Letters of Truth* (blog), November 4, 2004. https://www.eatpraybritney.com/lett ers-of-truth.

2   Spears, Britney. In the Zone Japan (press conference), December 12, 2003.

3   Smith, Ryan. "Why Britney Spears Shaved off Her Hair—Looking Back 15 Years Later." *Newsweek*, February 15, 2022. https://www.newsweek.com/why-britney-spears-shaved-off-her-hairlooking-back-15-years-later-1679388.

4   Archive-Farrah-Weinstein. "12 Ways For Britney To Get Her Groove Back." *MTV News*, November 30, 2006. https://www.mtv.com/news/1546890/12-ways-for-britney-to-get-her-groove-back/.

5   Sheffield, Rob. "Britney Phone Home: Why Spears' Telephone Beats Lady Gaga's by a Robo-Mile." *Rolling Stone* (blog), May 6, 2010. https://www.rollingstone.com/music/music-news/britney-phone-home-why-spears-telephone-beats-lady-gagas-by-a-robo-mile-243018/.

1

A Sicko Producer's Dream

In 2011, Nassima Abdelli-Beruh, a speech psychologist at Long Island University, conducted a study on the way teen girls talked. Abdelli-Beruh noticed that her students were speaking with "vocal fry," a raspy, deep tone caused by the slow fluttering of the vocal cords. She, along with some other speech psychologists, decided to investigate. She gathered thirty-four college girls to read aloud into a mic, and then assessed when and how long they slipped vocal fry into their sentences. The results didn't shock her. Abdelli-Beruh found that two-thirds of the women she tested used vocal fry, a slightly larger number than she thought.

Yet this finding was enough to unleash a torrent of think pieces about this apparently dangerous teen trend. According to the over-forty pundits that pumped out these scaremongering op-eds, vocal fry was annoying, unlistenable, and maybe even damaging to the vocal cords. Combined with "uptalk" and filler words, vocal fry made women easier to dismiss, less likely to get jobs, and unable to command respect. According to Hofstra fine arts professor emerita Laurie Fendrich, vocal fry and the "Valley Girl lift," "reveals an unexplainable lack of confidence in one's opinions and a radical uncertainty about one's place in the world."[1] Although uptalk and vocal fry are different sounds, impossible to use at the same time, Fendrich links them together—to her, they are equally annoying. These tics make women sound like "an empty-headed clotheshorse for whom the mall represents the height of culture."[2]

Though critics were quick to condemn vocal fry, Abdelli-Beruh withheld judgment. She said, in an interview with *MSNBC*, "Anecdotally, vocal fry is judged to be annoying by those who are not as young as the college students we tested."[3] Though Abdelli-Beruh and her critics may have disagreed about the effects of vocal fry, they agreed about the trend's cause: pop music. Abdelli-Beruh noted: "My son, who is a teenager, listens to 92.3 NOW in NYC. I noticed the way the voice said 'NOW' on the radio [is] clearly glottal fry."[4] In fact, it seemed that these concerned citizens condemned vocal fry *because* it linked today's teenage girls with a new wave of valley-girl celebrities: Jessica Simpson, Paris Hilton, and, most infamously, Britney Spears.

On ". . .Baby One More Time" Britney Spears croaked out her first words, "Oh baby, baby," her light Louisiana drawl twisting "baby" into "Bay-bay." Her voice is thin, an effect heightened by the track's hyper-compressed vocals, and dips in and out of vocal fry, punctuating her high-pitched, nasal voice with a low flutter in the beginning and end of her tones.

Fans and critics alike wondered if this voice was put on. Early tapes of Britney sound almost completely different.

On *Star Search*, she belted "Love Can Build a Bridge" in a preternaturally deep voice despite her tiny ten-year-old frame. On *The Mickey Mouse Club*, where she got her start, she sang the Staple Singers's "I'll Take You There," in her natural contralto (before her future boyfriend and fellow Mouseketeer Justin Timberlake emerged, rapping, inexplicably, in patois). For her auditions with record labels, Britney chose difficult songs to show off her powerhouse voice: two Whitney Houston songs ("I Will Always Love You" and "I Have Nothing,") and the national anthem.

Britney's song choices reflected the pop landscape of the late 1990s, where Toni Braxton and Mariah Carey reigned, and labels were looking for divas of their own to compete. In this context, Britney was something of an oddity. She came into Jive Records's bland offices wearing a sundress, and her demo tape came attached with photos of her smiling in pigtails, evoking her status as a Louisiana teen queen. Even weirder, her deep voice seemed totally at odds with her girlish demeanor. But Jive A&R Steve Lunt saw something in Britney: "When her voice went up high," he said, "You could hear the girlish quality, and there was something really appealing about that."

Even though Britney's high register was only part of her range, this "girlish quality" was what signed her. While Jive was predominantly a rap and R&B label (their roster included Aaliyah and A Tribe Called Quest), they didn't sign "artists like Whitney or Mariah"—Black pop divas—because they were, according to industry stereotypes, "expensive and risky," which, as Eric Beall told pop reporter John Seabrook, was the position of Clive Calder, co-founder of Jive. Britney, however, was a nice white girl who wanted to defer to authority, no questions asked. Chuck Yerger, Britney's tutor on the *Mickey Mouse Club*, said this about the starlet: "In all that she did, Britney gave the distinct impression that if an adult says do something, you do it. She truly felt that all adults and people in authority were good people, who had her best interests at heart."[5] This quality made her easier to mold into something that could sell. She was dirt-cheap to sign and eager to please. She conceded to a "get-out" deal, giving her label the ability to cancel her contract within ninety days, and Jive got to work on creating a voice that could make her famous.

Jive scrambled to find the right songwriter for Britney—they had plenty of producers for rappers and R&B artists, but, as Seabrook reports, just one that specialized in pop, Eric Foster White. White and the label folks decided to pass Britney along to someone with whom they had worked with on a few tracks for the Backstreet Boys: a young Swedish songwriter named Max Martin. Martin was affiliated with Swedish pop super-studio Cheiron, and had a song in mind for Britney—a slinky track called ". . .Baby One More Time." "Max, at that point in his career, thought he was writing an R&B song," Jive A&R rep Steve Lunt recalled, "whereas, in reality, he was writing a Swedish pop song. It was ABBA with a groove, basically." Because of Martin's proximity to pop, and perhaps even because of his white toe-dipping in Black aesthetics, Jive set him up with Britney. Lunt recalled that Martin took the project because: "[Britney's] fifteen years old; I can make the record I really want to make, and use her qualities appropriately, without her telling me what to do."[6] The first "quality" he took advantage of were Britney's vocals: in order to get to a sexy register while retaining her sweetness, Britney sang at a higher pitch but wrapped her words in vocal fry to imbue her voice with a moaning texture. Britney told *Rolling Stone* in 2000, "I wanted my voice to be kind of rusty. I wanted my voice to just be able to groove with the track. So the night before, I stayed up really, really late, so when I went into the studio, I wasn't rested."[7]

"...Baby One More Time" became an instant hit and, after a couple of months, launched Britney to the top of the charts. Martin continued to produce on Britney's subsequent albums, "...Baby One More Time," "Oops!... I Did It Again" and *Britney*, keeping her voice sweet and squeaky for cute ballads like "Sometimes" and turning up the rustiness for sexy numbers like *Oops!... I Did It Again*. This burbling sweet-and-sexy quality became Britney's trademark. Producers on her next albums manipulated her voice in the same way that Martin did—warping it to suit their purposes and develop their styles. Nowhere was this more clear than her 2003 album *In the Zone*, which was, at that point, her most experimental record. Producing teams Bloodshy and Avant, RedZone, and The Matrix stretched her voice to fit the disparate genres that they tried to emulate over the course of the album. On "Toxic," "Breathe on Me," and "Everytime" Britney sings, singing in thin, airy falsetto. On "Outrageous" and "Showdown" Britney raps in sultry whispers, and on "Shadow" she belts a heartbreaking ballad. Some of these experiments pay off. "Toxic," in particular, shows off Britney's range—her feathery high register, her robotic valley-girl growl, her strong, pleading belt. Others don't quite land, particularly when she dips her toe into historically Black genres, like the reggae-inflected "The Hookup," where she hazards a cringe-inducing patois. The album is an eclectic mix, evidence of an artist trying different styles on for size.

Though *In the Zone* contains some of Britney's best songs, many critics tore it apart. The main issue they had with it was her voice. *Rolling Stone*'s review notes, "Her voice is so processed, its physicality almost disappears ... Beyond the glittering beats, Spears sounds about as intimate as a blowup doll."[8] Other critics of *In the Zone* also critiqued Britney's vocal style using the language of sexual objectification: *Entertainment Weekly* describes her "pinched, porn-videogame delivery" as being so dehumanizing that she became nothing more than "a moaning, groaning, giggling sound effect."[9] These descriptions make Britney sound like a fleshlight that sings. They echo a 2000 interview with experimental musician Diamanda Galás, in which she said: "She doesn't even sound human! This is a producer's dream—a sicko producer's dream ... she sounds like a radioactive worm and she just crawls right under your skin."[10] To critics, Britney's constantly shifting voice made her seem vacant and spineless, an empty vessel waiting to be filled with her producers' ideas. Her voice was a symptom of her passivity, the same sweet girlishness that Steve Lunt noticed when she sang in Jive's New York conference room for the first time, the complete deference to authority Chuck Yerger saw in his classroom on the Disney lot.

But why interpret Britney's shifting voice as evidence of her exploitation? You could just as easily argue that it demonstrates her range, her creativity, or her willingness to experiment. If anything, footage of her in the studio suggests she had a collaborative, convivial relationship with the musicians who worked alongside her. She wasn't a doormat by any means. Max Martin has frequently called her a "genius," a creative powerhouse in her own right. Moreover, Britney, thankfully, does not seem to have suffered any abuse at the hands of her producers. So why did critics continue to impose this metaphor of sexual exploitation onto her music?

These criticisms of Britney's voice had more to do with the state of pop music in the early aughts than with her producers, or even Britney herself. In the 2000s, pop underwent its own industrial revolution, where teams of songwriters, producers, and label execs constructed hits, passing them from star to star as if they were on an assembly line. Producers became titans of the music industry—they often composed the songs, selected the sounds, and directed studio sessions. As producers took over pop, critics wondered what pop stars brought to the music, if anything at all. As music journalist John Seabrook put it in *The Song Machine*: "The artists occupy a central place in the songs, but more as vocal personalities than singers. The voices belong to real human beings, for the most part, although in some cases the vocals are so decked out in electronic finery that it doesn't matter whether a human or a machine made them."[11]

No one defined this new, producer-driven era in pop more than Max Martin. From 2010 to 2011, Martin's Katy Perry songs spent sixty-nine consecutive weeks in the Billboard

Top 10. As of now, Martin has twenty-five number-one hits, more than any other pop producer.

Before Martin, pop usually had a soulful, even meandering sensibility. The big hits from Mariah Carey and Toni Braxton feature vocal flourishes—ad-libs, over-dubs, and runs that make the vocal melody hard to pick up on a first listen. Martin's songs couldn't be more different. Fans and critics often describe his style as formulaic; the man himself called songwriting "like science to me." Martin's addictive melodies allowed no room for improvisation. His lyrics aren't exactly poetry— they have the sloppy uncanniness of mass-market English T-shirts in another country (like Ariana Grande's: "Now that I've become who I really are" or the Backstreet Boys's "Add on my uncanny ego/No one's less humbled than I"). But despite these grammatical errors, Martin crafts these lyrics syllable by syllable, making each line exactly symmetrical.

Martin also became famous for his affection for comping, the process in which a producer listens to every syllable of each vocal take and then strings together the strongest fragments to produce an flawless vocal performance. Comping is known to be dull, but Dr. Luke, Martin's mentee, told John Seabrook at the *New Yorker* that "Max loves comping. He'll do it for hours."[12] Martin is, by all accounts, a control freak: "I want to be part of every note, every single moment going on in the studio," Martin told the *Los Angeles Times* in a rare interview in 2000. "The producer should decide what kind of music is being made, what it's going to sound like—all of it, the why, when and how."[13]

While most pop producers made their careers working as hired guns for established acts, Martin preferred digging for unknowns—like Britney Spears in 1999—whom he could transform into stars. There was financial incentive for this strategy. Finding young, inexperienced starlets allows producers to exert greater control over the recording of the songs and to take a bigger cut of royalties by securing production rights that a more established performer wouldn't sign away. Before Martin and his protege, Dr. Luke, took them under their wings, the biggest pop idols of the 2010s were just getting their bearings in the music industry: Katy Perry was a blonde Christian folk-rock singer, Ke$ha was a high schooler with a country twang who nearly aced the SATs, and Kelly Clarkson had just won American Idol. Martin and Luke wrote songs for this cadre of white girls that teetered on the edge of sexuality and innocence, just like Martin designed for Britney. Though Katy Perry was an adult when she began her pop career, her songs ooze juvenile sexuality, filled with candy canes and cherry ChapStick and games of spin-the-bottle. Ke$ha's bratty talk-rap is certainly smutty, but it also feels childish, her brags about "brushing her teeth with a bottle of Jack" or letting boys "touch her junk" sounding like a kid who just learned to swear.

Defined by his obsessive control in and out of the studio, Martin brought back a tradition epitomized by Phil Spector, of the pop producer-as-auteur. Like Martin, Spector worked with a variety of vocalists and session musicians, but unlike Martin, Spector blatantly disregarded the contributions of the artists that worked for him. For example, The Ronettes had unsuccessfully sued Spector for unpaid royalties twice; in 2010, they banded together with Darlene Love and finally won. Spector famously said, at Ike Turner's funeral, that any number of backing singers "could have been Tina Turner," the chanteuse behind "River Deep, Mountain High."

Martin isn't as callous as Spector. But one can imagine, if Spector had access to Protools, he would have approached production in a similar way, carrying his auteurism to the digital sphere through techniques like comping and vocal processing.

Even though Martin was a cordial, respectful producer, Spector represented critics' worst fears about Martin's style of production, that, with the precedent of Spector, Martin's control-freak impulses would have dangerous consequences for the young women he worked with, including Britney.

Spector's monomaniacal control in the studio went hand in hand with his abuse of the young female starlets he worked with: at best he threatened to kill them, at worst he actually went through with it. In some ways, these critics were right to be scared. Though Martin himself has no reported history of abuse, in 2014, Kesha Rose Sebert (styled Ke$ha) sued Martin's protege, Dr. Luke, for sexual assault and battery, among other claims. Her accusations stemmed from an alleged incident in October 2005, shortly after she signed a contract with Luke, and several years before her chart-topper "TiK ToK" launched her career into the stratosphere. She said that after a night of partying, Luke handed her what he called "sober pills" and then raped her while she was unconscious. Afterwards, Luke subjected her to long-term emotional abuse and fat-shaming, which in turn, according to the lawsuit, caused "severe depression, post-traumatic stress, social isolation, and panic attacks."

Her account fused sexual abuse with Luke's control over her career. In September of 2013, a Kesha fan set up a petition to "free" Kesha from Dr. Luke's management, and accused Luke of "stunting" the singer's creative growth. The petition received over 10,000 signatures. It was later revealed in the documentary series *Ke$ha: My Crazy Beautiful Life*, that she had little creative control over her second album, *Warrior*, and had also stated that "Machine Gun Love," the song she felt most proud of, was omitted from the record against her wishes. According to fan sites, Kesha had written over seventy songs that were intended for *Warrior*, but Dr. Luke scrapped many of them. Kesha asked a judge to free her from her recording contract with Luke's Sony Music imprint Kemosabe Records because of his sexual abuse, but, unable to provide evidence for a rape that happened so long ago, she accused him of a hate crime, as a way to encapsulate the professional, sexual, and emotional harm she experienced. He was acquitted, because, according to the judge on the case: "Not every rape is a gender-motivated hate crime."[14]

Not only did Dr. Luke get off scot-free, but he also seemed to seek revenge. In 2016, Kesha had texted Lady Gaga about a rumor that Dr. Luke had assaulted Katy Perry, which turned out to be untrue. When Luke caught wind of the conversation, he obtained the texts, allegedly leaked them himself, sued Kesha for defamation, and won.

Dr. Luke was able to claim defamation precisely because he rejected fame and sought power behind the scenes instead. Dr. Luke isn't a household name, and therefore cannot legally be a "public figure," making it much easier for Luke's team to prove defamation. The court ruled that while Dr. Luke might be known in certain music circles, he had never "achieved general pervasive fame," nor had he "ever injected himself into the public debate about sexual assault or abuse of artists in the entertainment community."[15]

If he wanted to avoid "inject[ing] himself into the public debate about sexual assault," he shouldn't have raped someone. But the court didn't see it that way. Instead, the court thought that it was reasonable for Kesha to spend years of her adult life and hundreds of thousands of dollars dragging an unwitting producer into the public spectacle of #MeToo, just because she wanted a more lucrative contract. The court found it inconceivable that Kesha, eighteen years old, still woozy from the "sober pill" she had taken the night before, had called her mom instead of getting a rape kit. They could not believe that she felt powerless against the man who controlled her music, her career, and even her body, and did not go public with her accusation immediately after it happened. They sided with him. Because Kesha is the "public figure," they decided she must pay the price for her own abuse.

Kesha's case represents the worst possible version of the Svengali-producer teen-starlet relationship that originated with Britney and came to define aughts teen-pop. Her contract suspended her in a perpetual state of adolescence. Unable to release new music, we still see her as a bratty teen with disheveled hair and feathered eyeliner, drunkenly bragging about a new crush. Even as a thirty-something, every song she writes has to be approved by her abuser before its release. In her music, she can refer to her traumas only through innuendo, as in her song "Prayer," where she sings about an unnamed "you" who "put [her] through hell." Meanwhile, Dr. Luke still profits off of Kesha's music, even the songs that explore the effects of his abuse. He continues to work. He can be well-known when he wants to be, collecting royalty checks from his many hits, and disappearing when it becomes a legal or financial burden. In 2020, he was nominated for a Grammy for his work on Doja Cat's "Say So" under a pseudonym.

Years before Kesha's assault, critics projected these long-standing fears about the exploitative nature of pop music onto Britney. They assumed, correctly, that the ruthlessness of the pop machine disempowered stars to such a degree that emotional and sexual abuse could run rampant, as in the case of Kesha and Dr. Luke. But shrouding these concerns in criticism of Britney's "robotic" voice was a subtle form of victim-blaming. The implication was that her producers took advantage of her because she made it too easy. From afar, it seemed that Britney accepted the demands of her producers and managers with a smile, no matter what those demands may have been. If they wanted her to be slutty, she'd take her clothes off and swivel her hips, and if they wanted her to be a cute little girl, she'd put on a purity ring and go to church. By refusing to assert her voice, neither literally nor figuratively, so the logic goes, she not only invited her own abuse but also created the expectation that other young pop stars should keep sweet even in a system that harms them.

No wonder middle-aged pundits got so concerned about Britney's vocal fry. Britney's voice primed her for exploitation, they thought, and their daughters were talking just like her.

***

Like ". . .Baby One More Time," *Blackout* opens with a sound bite from Britney. But instead of a coquettish come-on, Britney announces herself—"It's Britney, Bitch"—in a low, scarily mechanical tone, before giggling and fading into the synths. In the song that follows, "Gimme More," Britney sounds like a broken robot, glitching and sputtering through the song. As she sings about the difficulties of escaping the public eye in a darkened club, her voice begins to splinter. A low, hyper-processed voice repeats the ends of the verses, like an echo. On the chorus, she repeats "gimme gimme," and different versions of her voice end the phrase with "more" pitched up, pitched down, warped into a breathy squeak. The voices multiply throughout the outro, which lasts two-and-a-half minutes, almost half the song. Britney riffs over the chorus, as different robotic voices stutter and croon interweaving hooks.

Then a deep male voice comes in: "Bet you didn't see this one coming . . . the legendary Miss Britney Spears, and the unstoppable Danja." He ends the song ominously: "You gonna have to remove me, cause I ain't going nowhere." This voice is Nate "Danja" Hills, the producer of over half of *Blackout*.

It might seem arrogant for Danja, producing on his own for the first time, to introduce himself on the same level as Britney. In fact, Danja's voice is on almost every track he produced for *Blackout*, introducing her on "Perfect Lover," or answering her in a call-and-response on "Hot as Ice." In "Get Naked (I've Got a Plan)," Britney doesn't even sing the chorus, deferring entirely to Danja. Danja took Britney's voice and multiplied it, clipped it, slowed it down, and compressed it until it no longer sounded human, treating Britney as another midi instrument to manipulate. Throughout the album, her vocals are mixed so that they fade into the synths, in the same way that it's hard to hear a friend in a club even if they're shouting as loud as they can. This effect is disquieting and distancing. As Kelefa Sanneh put it in his review of *Blackout* in *The New York Times*: Britney "managed to become a spectral presence—on her own album."

Danja's trajectory as a producer seemed to indicate that he was a monomaniacal auteur like Max Martin, prepared to mold Britney's voice to whatever he needed. Danja rose up the pop food chain in the early aughts as the protege of one of the decade's most influential producers: Timothy Mosely, known commonly as Timbaland. If Max Martin was one model of auteurist pop producer, Timbaland was another. In keeping with Martin's elusive nature, his talent was constructing the foundation of a track—the structure, the hooks—rather than its surface details. This made Martin particularly adaptable. Though he started in bubblegum teen pop, his sound changed with the times, incorporating trendy details like dubstep drops and rapped verses into his signature ear-worm hits. Though he may have had monomaniacal control over his tracks, Martin crafted them precisely so you won't hear him.

Meanwhile, you know a Timbaland production when you hear one. He populates his beats with idiosyncratic details that you wouldn't find anywhere else: the funky-croak bassline on Ginuwine's "Pony," the baby squeaking on Aaliyah's "Are You

That Somebody," the elephant trumpet and revving backward speech on Missy Elliot's "Work It." Timbaland curates these samples to create textured, off-kilter beats. His beats start and stop like a car with a broken ignition, punctuating a moment of silence with an eardrum-shattering 808. He seeds sounds from his vast library—Middle Eastern string samples, beat boxing, synth hiccups—into his tracks to create a sound that was uniquely his.

While Timbaland's pop persona rose and rose, Danja was a kid in Virginia Beach, slipping mixtapes of his beats to anyone that would listen. He taught himself to loop beats and saved up money to get a $300 Casio console from his part-time job at Burger King. He inserted himself in the scene in Virginia Beach, the birthplace of Missy Elliot, Pharrell, and Timbaland himself. Larry Live, Timbaland's best friend, introduced the two in 2001 after a conference in Virginia Beach. Later that evening, the two ran into each other again at a party. Tim said some sweet nothings, saying he'd be happy to pass the torch to Danja. Two years later, the two ran into each other again, and Danja wouldn't let this opportunity go to waste. A nervous 22-year-old Danja sat in Tim's tour bus and played some of his tracks off a CD he burned. Tim was impressed; he "went crazy" according to Danja. From that moment forward Timbaland viewed him as a full-on partner.

It's not hard to hear why. Timbaland had previously been a sample-driven producer, rarely writing melodies, letting the singers and songwriters he collaborated with riff on top of his strange, hypnotic beats. But once Danja and Timbaland formed their partnership, they co-produced two pop smashes, Justin Timberlake's *Futuresex/Lovesounds* and Nelly Furtado's *Loose*. Danja's chords and keyboard melodies anchor many of the hit songs from these records, including Furtado's "Promiscuous" and Timberlake's "Summer Love." Danja had a particular ear for instrumental hooks, which were becoming increasingly important to Tim, as he was trying to conquer pop just as he had conquered R&B.

They started working together in 2003, first for smaller names like recent Tim signee John Doe, then for bigger stars like Nelly Furtado and Justin Timberlake. Just listening to the results, you can hear their process: Tim would craft a layered beat, and Danja would add synth chords. Danja's most notable contribution was to Justin Timberlake's 2006 album *Futuresex/Lovesounds*, in which he introduced trance beats to Tim's typical R&B productions. "I heard dance and techno and was always interested in it but didn't really know where to go. But I went to a club one night and saw that people were losing their mind to these dance tracks," Danja told *Vibe* in 2011.[16] "It wasn't really that I wanted to mimic that sound. I just wanted to have that energy and have people going crazy. So I knew the fusion was putting R&B with trance. As soon as I put the 'boom boom kat', I *knew* it." *Futuresex/Lovesounds* was a critical and commercial hit, and the album put Danja on the map as one of the most innovative producers working in pop.

By 2007, after four years working for Tim, Danja was ready to step out of Timbaland's shadow. It already seemed that he was going in that direction anyway; Scott Storch, a collaborator-turned-rival of Timbaland, wrote a diss track about the famous producer, in which he rapped: "Your boy

Danja got to hate you with a passion, man/He makes the hits while you taking all the credit, damn." When Britney's A&R offered Danja the opportunity to produce solo on *Blackout*, he took it.

At the time, pop producers were usually hired guns, stepping into the studio to draft only one or two songs on any given record. Online, listeners tended to purchase individual songs rather than albums, so producers focused on creating attention-grabbing singles. As a result, albums sounded like an eclectic mix that never really fit together. Though Danja flourished in this system, he saw himself as an old-fashioned album artist, an auteur not unlike Martin or his mentor. "An album should be like a book: It should have one story," he told the *Wall Street Journal* in 2007.[17] He approached *Blackout* as a complete sonic project, one which would establish his career just as much as it could bring back Britney's. He inserted his voice into "Gimme More," he said, because, "I just felt like I needed to say something. People haven't really seen me or heard my voice, and that was one of my first solo productions. So I definitely had to stake my claim."[18] Danja produced most of *Blackout*'s songs, and established its signature nightmarish electro-pop sound.

On *Blackout*, Danja was left to his own devices, alongside fellow producer Jim Beanz and composer Keri Hilson. Alone in the studio, they built tracks that Britney could sing over whenever she could show up. They didn't know when Britney would come in, or for how long. In an interview with the *Fader*, Keri Hilson reflected: "She did not write on any of the songs that we did—we would create, and I would lay a demo while we awaited her arrival." She continued, "When we played her my demo of 'Break the Ice', she didn't want to do the background. Honestly, I think she said something like, 'it sounds like me anyway.'"[19]

These factors made *Blackout* seem like Britney's *most* extreme deference to her producers so far, even more extreme than in *In the Zone* or her Max Martin albums. Viewed through the least charitable lens, one could argue that Danja took advantage of Britney's absence, using her star power to further his own career. Critics echoed this sentiment. They liked *Blackout*, but thought that the album's strengths had nothing to do with Britney. The things that made *Blackout* great, they argued—wry lyrics and forward-looking production—were the results of her all-star writers and producers, who wrote the songs, crafted layered beats, and manipulated her voice until it was basically unrecognizable. *Rolling Stone* called the album's producers "a VIP list of puppet-masters." As Sasha Frere-Jones put it for the *New Yorker*: "The new Britney Spears album, *Blackout*, is good the way the Yankees are good. If you have enough money, you can buy more talent than the other guys."[20] Music critics reviewed *Blackout* like a food critic would review an Oreo: it's good, but only because it was designed to be as commercially palatable as possible.

Blackout may have presented a confident Britney, but this was a mirage, according to her critics. Caroline Sullivan most explicitly expressed this attitude in an op-ed for the *Guardian* titled "Don't give Britney credit where it isn't due." In the piece, she warned listeners not to think of Britney as *Blackout*'s author: "Spears is not a musician, or even a 'singer,' as such ... She's not of the class of artists who funnel their despair into their art, and shouldn't be applauded as such."[21] To Sullivan, Britney had hit rock bottom, not just because she was a trainwreck, but because she was unable to transfigure it into art. She may have been a dutiful performer, an "entertainer," but in light of her breakdown, she couldn't even manage that. To her critics, *Blackout* represented the darkest vision of Britney's career, fulfilling their worst fears about the direction of pop music. The pop stars are arbitrary—when Britney fails, there will be another girl primed to replace her, whose producers can transform her most banal experiences into a song that can be consumed by millions, then forgotten.

It seemed that, in contrast to the 1990s, in which grunge, and the counterculture spirit it represented, ruled the charts, aughts pop music represented a return to a world in which songs were products rather than art. But it seems facile, even naive, to suggest that one can draw the line between art and commerce so easily. Singing about the counterculture does not a revolutionary make, and the market can profit off anything with a pulse. Still, this account of pop music is seductive. It transforms the fraught, cyclical relationship between art and capitalism into a story with heroes and villains—the vapid innocent starlet, preyed on by her evil label, versus the tortured producer who is attempting to make art in a system that only values money.

But this narrative reaffirms sexist stereotypes of who can truly be considered an artist. Though critics dismissed the pop machine as soul-sucking and corrupt, they lauded Timbaland and Max Martin and even Danja as geniuses who were able to thrive even in a flawed system. When it came to the stars themselves, who were, more often than not, women, they were less charitable. There was always a way to discount Britney's agency, even on albums where she was more involved in the songwriting process. Her vocal delivery was always strange and surprising, in addition to demonstrating technical skill, but she was rarely credited for these contributions. Instead, they were treated as accidents, or products of her producers' manipulation. This paradigm proffers a woman's life as raw material that a man must transform into art; that any woman in the spotlight has a man behind her pulling the strings.

Moreover, attributing a song to a single author seems willingly ignorant of the way pop music is actually made, and removes credit from the many people that shape an album's sound, from studio engineers to session musicians to the star herself. *Blackout* foregrounds pop's collaborative spirit, staging a dialogue between Britney and her producers in the music itself. One of the key aesthetic qualities of *Blackout* is a multiplicity of voices. Though Danja features his voice prominently on the record, he's just one of many voices weaving around Britney's. Other producers announce their presence, like Sean "The Pen" Garrett, who introduces "Toy Soldier" with: "Yeah, smash on the radio, bet I penned it." But often, Danja manipulates vocal tracks so flagrantly that it's difficult to identify who's singing. Choruses of voices intertwine around Britney's on Danja's productions, from "Break the Ice" to "Gimme More," including male voices and even Britney herself, pitched down until she sounds unrecognizable. She almost never sings a chorus alone. She cedes center stage to Danja on "Get Naked (I've Got a Plan)" or lets her voice drop out on "Hot as Ice," letting a crew of voices answer her in a call-and-response. Danja plays hype-man, getting Britney ready to sing. Britney provides her input, too, saying "I like this part" on "Break the Ice," or beckoning Danja to bring the beat back on after a quick pause in "Get Back." At the end of "Gimme More," Danja even shouts out the album's sound engineer, Marcella Araica, "The Incredible Lago." The music itself signals to listeners that this is not the result of a monomaniacal auteur pulling the strings, but rather a collaboration.

Danja has said, throughout his career, that the most important thing he can do as a producer is to create an atmosphere in the studio in which the artist would feel most comfortable. In a panel for Full Sail University, he said that he paid close attention to "set[ting] the mood for the writer or the artist or the producer, and leaving them in their creative space ... putting this person in the most comfortable atmosphere to be able to do their job."[22] He noted that Timbaland liked to begin work at 1 a.m., while Missy Elliott wanted Danja to work superhumanly fast. But Britney was different. The way she tapped into her confidence was through dance. "You would know how she felt about a song by pure body language; she didn't have to say anything," he reflected to the *Fader*. "She would still be nailing the lyrics and the melody, but she would be in there really dancing. You hear stories of Michael Jackson doing full-on choreography while recording some of his songs and it was the same thing with her. I was just making sure I made grooves that she could dance to, something hard and edgy with hip-hop undertones. Once I realized that was what she wanted to do, that's where I stayed."[23] Keri Hilson recalled to the *Fader*, "We were given the specific direction that she did not want the music to mimic her personal life. So we figured, 'OK, so let's create a fantasy world that she would be happy in."[24]

So Danja and his collaborators created an ethereal space in which Britney could escape the pressures of performing her public persona and melt into the euphoria of the club. This space allowed Britney to blossom. In the studio, Britney was not a wild child or a pushover or a prima donna; she was a professional. Though critics painted her as vacant and absent from the songwriting process, her producers tell a different story. Keri Hilson reflected: "Even if we only got two hours of her, which would be the case some days ... She takes it so [seriously], and an artist that takes themselves seriously has to acknowledge when they are unable to give their 100 percent that day, to protect their art. I respect that so much more than an artist who would come in and bullshit you." Danja felt similarly, saying "Throughout the whole process, she was very present, attentive, and interactive. She was one of the easiest people to get things done with—she would sit there and sing no matter how many times we had her do it over, and just get it done."[25] Danja and Hilson recast Britney's can-do attitude as an empowering, professional quality rather than a result of her passivity.

Throughout Britney's career, critics and fans have proposed opposing views of Britney's voice, both her literal singing voice and her "voice" as a metaphor for her artistic point of view. Some suggest that Britney's voice is inauthentic, a studio product, a symptom of her deference to manipulative producers and label reps. Others see her voice as a technical marvel, a product of her unflinching artistic vision that her producers diligently execute. Though these narratives seem mutually exclusive, they're both present in *Blackout*. On all of *Blackout*'s tracks, Britney's voice is simultaneously unmistakable and auto-tuned beyond recognition, just as the album shows off her fuck-you, punk-rock spirit alongside her willingness to self-deprecate and defer to others' authority.

Danja's approach to production allows us to look beyond these narratives to create a more complex account of Britney's artistry. No one can take full responsibility for *Blackout*'s unique sound. Instead, Danja and his colleagues fostered a collaborative atmosphere that allowed her a safe space to explore, vital during a tumultuous time in her personal life. In keeping with this experimental spirit, Danja allowed Britney's voice to be unpredictable and out of control. On *Blackout*, Britney's a vocal texture, an ad-lib, a giggle. Britney's voice on *Blackout* creaks and croaks and whispers. It's treated like a sample: chopped-and-screwed, slowed down, and sped back up. This approach is no less artificial than Max Martin's syllable-by-syllable manipulation, but the difference is that the voices on *Blackout* were *meant* to sound inhuman and interrupted. *Blackout* doesn't privilege a "real," unfiltered Britney—there is no flawless vocal take nor perfect syllable worth comping together.

Critics of Britney's voice dismiss her textures as "artificial" or "inauthentic," as if she were hiding some real voice underneath the expressive layers, just as critics of vocal fry worry that young women conceal their true selves behind an annoying, unlistenable affect. These concerns about Britney's voice and the women who emulate her conceal a deeper fear of white women rejecting social and cultural power. There's a reason that middle-aged pundits focalize their concerns about vocal fry onto white girls. White women are taught that they can escape their own exploitation if they play by the rules. Britney embodied this fantasy. She commanded sexual, financial, and cultural power by being sweet, sultry, and non-threatening. But this relative social mobility is conditional. When people took issue with Britney's voice, it was a warning. If you want to have a voice, it must be pleasant to listen to. It can't make you seem stupid or submissive, promiscuous or fake. So much misogyny takes the form of a catch-22: you have to conform to societal expectations while being "authentically" yourself, perform flawlessly without putting in any effort. Your voice is both how you seem and who you are. It better be good enough.

But the only reason that you have to "find your voice" in the first place is so people can know, immediately, if you're worth listening to. Britney developed her voice literally overnight because she had to sell it. The high-pitched gravelly voice she created for ". . .Baby One More Time" worked, and it stuck. Is it real? I don't know if it is the voice she would have given herself had she never stepped foot in the Jive offices in 1997. I don't know if it's how she talks when she's with the people she loves, how she sings to herself when no one's around.

It doesn't have to be. *Blackout* reminds us that no one has just one voice. On *Blackout*, Britney could sound like anything. *Blackout* shoves her most controversial vocal tics right into listeners' ears, playing up her voice's affectless, artificial tinge. Danja imitates her throughout the album—in the chorus of "Gimme More," there's a voice chanting "more" that's drenched in vocal fry, and on "Get Naked (I Got a Plan)" Danja growls a low "ahhh" that flutters the vocal cords as a form of percussion. On *Blackout*, vocal fry isn't treated as a way to distinguish Britney in the market or a reason to exploit her or a sin. It's a sound. Like all sounds, it hangs in the air for a second, and fades away.

Notes

1 The Chronicle of Higher Education. "The Valley-Girl Lift." March 12, 2010. https://www.chronicle.com/blogs/brainstorm/the-valley-girl-lift.

2 Ibid.

3 NBC News. "More College Women Speak in Creaks, Thanks to Pop Stars." December 12, 2011. http://www.nbcnews.com/healthmain/more-college-women-speak-creaks-thanks-pop-stars-1C6436911.

4 "More College Women Speak in Creaks, Thanks to Pop Stars."

5 Dennis, Steve. *Britney: Inside the Dream—The Biography*. London: HarperCollins Publishers Limited, 2009.

6 Seabrook, John. The Song Machine: Inside the Hit Factory. W. W. Norton & Company, 87, 2015.

7 Sheffield, Rob. "How Britney Spears Changed Pop with 'Baby One More Time.'" *Rolling Stone* (blog), January 12, 2019. https://www.rollingstone.com/feature/britney-spears-baby-one-more-time-anniversary-rob-sheffield-777564/.

8 Pareles, Jon. "In the Zone." *Rolling Stone* (blog), November 19, 2003. https://www.rollingstone.com/music/music-album-reviews/in-the-zone-89839/.

9 David Browne, "In the Zone." EW.com, November 21, 2003. https://ew.com/article/2003/11/21/zone-0/.

10 Galas, Diamanda "Oops. . .I Did It Again," Time Out NY, August 2000.

11 Seabrook, John. The Song Machine.

12 Seabrook, John. "The Doctor Is In." *The New Yorker*. October 7, 2013. https://www.newyorker.com/magazine/2013/10/14/the-doctor-is-in.

13 Boucher, Geoff. "Practicing the Fine Art of Production." Los Angeles Times, June 4, 2000. https://www.latimes.com/archives/la-xpm-2000-jun-04-ca-37230-story.html.

14 Kornhaber, Spencer. "The Legal Facts about Kesha's Loss." The Atlantic, April 7, 2016. https://www.theatlantic.com/entertainment/archive/2016/04/kesha-dismissal-statute-of-limitations-dr-luke/477261/.

15 Rosenbaum, Claudia. "Kesha Dealt Stunning Blow in Dr. Luke's $50M Defamation Lawsuit." *Billboard* (blog), February 7, 2020. https://www.billboard.com/pro/kesha-dr-luke-50m-defamation-lawsuit/.

16 Hova, Tray. "Studio Stories: Danja [Pg. 2]." *VIBE.Com* (blog), February 7, 2011. https://www.vibe.com/news/entertainment/studio-stories-danja-pg-2-44595/.

17 Jurgensen, John. "Life of Danja." *Wall Street Journal*, October 14, 2007, sec. Leisure/Weekend. https://www.wsj.com/articles/SB119223062349357914.

18 The FADER. "10 Years of Blackout: Britney Spears, Her Favorite Collaborators, and Fans, Celebrate the Best Pop Album Ever." n. d. https://www.thefader.com/2017/09/27/britney-spears-blackout-interview-10-year-anniversary-2007.

19 Ibid.

20 Frere-Jones, Sasha. "Buyout." *The New Yorker*, August 12, 2008. http://www.newyorker.com/culture/sasha-frere-jones/buyout.

21 Sullivan, Caroline. "Don't Give Britney Credit Where It Isn't Due." *The Guardian*, December 31, 2007, sec. Music. https://www.theguardian.com/music/musicblog/2007/dec/31/dontgivebritneycreditwhere.

22 Araica, Marcella, and Hills, Nate. Timbaland to Timberlake: The Mixing Careers of Danja & Ms. Lago, March 1, 2013.

23 The FADER. "10 Years of Blackout."

24 Ibid.

25 Ibid.

2

Bimbos of the Apocalypse

In the music video for her 2004 song "Everytime," during the song's plaintive piano intro, Britney's limo zips down the Las Vegas Strip, before pulling up to the Palms Casino Resort. Once her vocals start, a swarm of paparazzi descends on her; fans hurl themselves at the car door. Unlike past videos, Britney barely lip-syncs to the song; the song serves as an emotional soundtrack to the video, the video committing the song's feelings to film. "Notice me," Britney sings on the track, as bodyguards ward off fans and paps.

Britney bolts out of the limo as guards manhandle her and force her through the ravenous crowd. When she gets up to her room, she and her boyfriend, a Kevin Federline look-alike, get into a fight, which escalates until stunt double K-Fed launches a vase full of flowers at the wall. Britney flees to the bathroom to soak in the tub, we think, to calm down. But in the middle of the video, she sinks into the water, as if to drown herself. The video fades to white. In the fade-in, Britney's in a hospital. She looks at a mother giving birth, longing to be reborn. We then flash back to Britney in the tub—it turns out the suicide was just fantasy. She surfaces and giggles, as if to reassure the viewer that it was all just a dream. There's something unnerving about how quickly she shakes off her sadness, as if her suicidal ideation could evaporate with a smile.

This isn't the first time that Britney explored in her music the effects of fame. In 2000, off of *Oops!... I Did It Again*, she released "Lucky," a Max Martin bubblegum tune about "a girl named Lucky," a "Hollywood girl," who still wonders, "If there's nothing missing in my life/then why do these tears come at night?" The similarities between "Lucky" and Britney herself proved both poignant and prescient, as the lyrics point to a growing dissatisfaction with her life in the spotlight. But the song teems with kitsch, from its faux doo-wop string sample to the music literally enacting what the lyrics describe (when Britney sings about a knock on the door, we hear three thumps). "Lucky" is so sickeningly sweet that it feels haunting. She can't quite articulate her sadness; the emptiness of her life is kept narrowly out of frame. She asks "why the tears come at night," but never gets a response.

Ever since she got famous, Britney Spears has been making music about it. The songs couldn't be more different: "Lucky" is a saccharine Motown pastiche, while "Everytime," is a self-serious piano ballad with Muzak strings and relatively unprocessed vocals, straining for authenticity. Both "Lucky" and "Everytime" treat fame as inherently destructive, but "Everytime's" video answers "Lucky's" rhetorical question by quite heavy-handedly suggesting that the tabloids torture Britney with both psychic and actual violence.

In 2008, she released a music video for the song, "Piece of Me," the second single off *Blackout*, which also explores the consequences of fame. We still start with a shot of the paparazzi, trying to get a good photo through Britney's window. But this time, she's flirting and posing at the mirror, getting ready for a night out with her girlfriends without paying mind to the paparazzi outside. One pap gets a shot of Britney inadvertently mooning the crowd, and we see the image on the cover of *The National Gossip* with the headline "Derriere on Display," which she tears in half. Instead of cowering and sulking, she courts the cameras when she wants to and flips them off when she doesn't. "You want a piece of me?" She sings. The implication is that you don't.

"Piece of Me" opens with a grungy synth pushing the song into gear, along with crunchy, distorted drums and a chopped-up moan. Rather than digitally pitch-correcting her, the auto-tune flattens her vocal affect into jaded boredom. Britney sings only two notes through the verses, as she seems to yawn over her unending scandals; the lyrics flow forward with almost no pauses. She sings about the paparazzi as a cautionary tale—even if she hits them with her Range Rover, she'll end up settling out of court for pocket change. "Another day, another drama," she snarls. The paparazzi don't make her weep or send her into a depressive spiral; now, she just rolls her eyes.

Britney recorded *Blackout* during her most intense years of public scrutiny. With paparazzi invading every aspect of her life, she could no longer just smile and wait for them to go away. By the time the "Piece of Me" video came out, her relationship with the press had become much more combative. She lashed out, flipping off the paparazzi one night. Her provocations grew in intensity: when asked how she was doing at a court hearing for the custody of her children, in October 2007, she told a pap to "eat it, lick it, snort it, fuck it." In a particularly infamous incident, she stole an umbrella from a pap that pissed her off and whacked his car with it.

But in "Piece of Me" Britney's not angry; she's ambivalent. Unlike in the "Everytime" and "Lucky" videos, where the tabloids push her to melodramatic lows, in "Piece of Me" she shrugs it off, worn down from her years in the spotlight but still finding moments of pleasure in its perverse thrills.

"Piece of Me" fits well with Danja's work on *Blackout*. He subverts the expectations of Top 40 pop by highlighting the ambiguity and artificiality of Britney's persona, manipulating Britney's voice and interrupting it with synth hits and vocal samples. But Danja didn't produce "Piece of Me;" instead, Bloodshy and Avant, a team of Swedish super-producers, penned the song. Like Danja, they play up the synthetic nature of Britney's persona, but they tie it to the mechanics of celebrity culture and the music industry much more explicitly. "Piece of Me's" lyrics create many different "Britneys," from "Miss Bad Media Karma" to Mrs. "Most Likely to Get on the TV For Strippin' on the Streets When Gettin' the Groceries." If you come for Britney, you don't know what Britney you're going to get: "Ms. American Dream" or Mrs. "You Want a Piece of Me." The title points to the consumptive relationship between Britney and the press—by demanding so much from her, they tear her into pieces. Both "Piece of Me" and *Blackout* as a whole, evoke and complicate Britney's relationship with the cruelty of celebrity culture in a way none of her work would again.

But it's unclear exactly what *Blackout* is trying to say about Britney's stardom. Some saw *Blackout*'s cynicism as evidence that Britney was reframing her scuffles with paparazzi as attempts to assert her agency over her public persona. Britney's team certainly seemed to cling to this interpretation of the record. Her label suggested that the title *Blackout* "refers to blocking out negativity and embracing life fully," which is, to put it mildly, a stretch. Since the release of "Piece of Me," Britney's team has seemed to double-down on this glibly optimistic interpretation of the track. Her smash-hit 2013 Vegas residency and ensuing tour, were both called "Piece of Me."

But when *Blackout* came out, it certainly didn't seem like Britney was in control, even if she shrugged off her many scandals. Critics lauded Britney for responding directly to her public snafus on "Piece of Me," but, like most songs on *Blackout*, Britney didn't write it. Most seemed to treat the confidence she displayed on the song as an anomaly, or even wishful thinking. In most of her public appearances, she seemed unhinged, her head shaved, her eyes wide with rage. Vanessa Grigoriadis, a reporter for *Rolling Stone*, wrote: "She is not a good girl. She is not America's sweetheart. She is an inbred swamp thing who chain-smokes, doesn't do her nails . . . and screams at people who want pictures for their little sisters."[1]

Blackout's relationship to celebrity culture is particularly hard to parse precisely because Britney was such a complicated figure at the time the record came out. Britney Spears came to represent the dream and nightmare of celebrity culture, the tabloid industry in its most maximal form. In 2007, Britney was the biggest star in the world, adored and hated in equal measure. She had been the most searched celebrity on *Yahoo* for three years straight, and images of her paid the salaries for an entire generation of paparazzi. But it's still unclear what made Britney so fascinating (and profitable) in the first place. The amount of scrutiny placed on Britney was not a foregone conclusion. Any number of starlets could have assumed the title of the celebrity meltdown du jour. Yet the spotlight remained on Britney. Open up an old copy of *Us Weekly* or log onto *TMZ* and find a never-ending stream of Britney images: she smiles and poses outside of the Ivy, exits a limo with her legs spread, floats out the door of some club, svelte and ethereal. It's not hard to find video footage of Britney weaving through a mass of people holding cameras bigger than their heads, as they scream at her, a deafening chorus of "hey Britney!" "Over here!" In these clips, sometimes even "We love you, Britney," sounds like a threat.

By the mid aughts, you could know about as much about a celebrity as you could know about your own friends. You could find out what celebrities bought at the gas station, where they celebrated their birthdays, the last times they cried. The nascent gossip blog *Gawker* even had a feature called "Gawker Stalker Maps," which allowed the user to pinpoint exactly where celebs were hanging out. The paparazzi, once reserved for red carpets, were everywhere. One could never tell whether a star would cooperate or bite back. It seemed to depend on their mood, mercurial as the weather. Guerrilla photographers frequently got into fistfights over a photo. Any shoot could turn into a bloodbath.

Some of the most startling footage of celebrity surveillance came from the paparazzi themselves. In 2010, a documentary premiered titled *Paparazzi: Full Throttle LA*, shot and edited by Daniel "Dano" Ramos, an infamous documentarian-turned-pap. Ramos was the guy who stalked Britney Spears to the outside of a Jiffy Lube, before she attacked him with an umbrella. In the film, Ramos has a gentle, soft-spoken demeanor, and an anthropological eye. He presents himself as a fish-out-of-water journalist looking to capture the high-octane world of the paparazzi, before getting sucked in by the money and the thrill of getting a good shot. In the documentary, he follows a few paps—Felix, Roberto, and Felipe—as they go about their work. They seem invested in the integrity of their trade, and are often protective of the stars they cover, having shadowed them for years. In a touching scene, Roberto herds a swarm of photographers away from a restaurant where a teenage Miley Cyrus eats lunch with a friend. "Give her some privacy," he yells. "This is what gives paparazzi a bad name." Still, there's only so much he can do—the paps chase her down the parking lot and follow her to her car.

Though the sharp increase in paparazzi photography made the aughts seem like a unique celebrity panopticon, this combative relationship between tabloids and celebrities have been a part of pop culture since the 1950s. *Confidential*, a gossip magazine founded by Robert Harrison, introduced many of these confrontational tactics. Harrison wanted to create a magazine that didn't pander to the stars with puff pieces, like the popular *Photoplay*. Instead, he published scandals and smut. This, understandably, made celebrities reluctant to work with him. To gather material for *Confidential*, Harrison commissioned private investigators and paid tipsters, along with photographers with the latest audio–visual technology— techniques that tabloids would also deploy at the turn of the twenty-first century. *Confidential*, relying on scattershot photos and tips, almost never told a full story about any particular event; instead, they'd drop whatever they had, and they would then update the story in subsequent issues. This transformed gossip into a soap opera, with endless cliffhangers and mysteries, where readers would have to buy the next issue to know what happened next. But *Confidential* couldn't last. Sales tanked, and it folded in 1978.

Paparazzi photos became increasingly important in the 1970s, as relatively new outlets like *National Enquirer* and *People* started transitioning from subscriptions to single-issue sales. Both magazines sustained themselves with impulse buys, over-the-supermarket-counter sales—this type of distribution comprised 90 percent of the *National Enquirer*'s sales in 1972. To make these issues attractive enough to compel a customer to pick up an issue, they needed sensational, attractive photos for their covers. But the industry couldn't support armies of guerrilla photographers, as they could in the 2000s. An individual paparazzo had to buy an expensive camera, miles of film, development, and distribution. Their jobs were in constant jeopardy, as celebrities could easily deny them access. If a celebrity turned down interviews with gossip magazines, there wasn't a whole lot the paparazzi could do to wring scandals out of them.

The changes to tabloid magazines in the late twentieth century—switching to single-issue sales and dropping tiny tidbits of a story at a time—set the stage for the paparazzi industry to inflate in the aughts. Both tactics relied on having a steady stream of splashy photos to keep readers hooked, which grew easier as sales (and therefore budgets) increased and digital photography became the norm. This expansion began when *Us Weekly* hired Bonnie Fuller as its editor-in-chief. Fuller's most genius invention was a recurring feature called "Stars: They're Just Like Us." Fuller realized that there was a market for photos of celebrities walking their dogs or heading to the local Starbucks for a cappuccino. *Us Weekly* quickly became a runaway newsstand hit. Concurrently with this rise in demand for even the most banal paparazzi images, it became increasingly easy and cheap to track a celebrity's daily life as digital cameras became more affordable. This encouraged paparazzi to shoot celebrities night and day, since any image could turn a profit. This new hunger for paparazzi images made *Us* magazine the subject of celebrity ire. Gwyneth Paltrow called Fuller "the Devil."

This demand for paparazzi photos only increased with the rise of gossip blogs, like *Perez Hilton, JustJared, Defamer, DListed*, and so on. These blogs operated entirely outside of the entertainment industry, and as such did not respect the gossip industry's manners and mores. Bloggers went full gonzo. They stole from paparazzi agencies, published unverified rumors, and leaked obscene and defamatory information. Perez Hilton was particularly flagrant. Perez simply used a photo when he wanted to, without respect for copyright laws or journalistic ethics. A blog, only concerned with garnering clicks almost always won the game of breaking celebrity news.

Web-based gossip outlets moved faster than weeklies ever could. *TMZ*, a gossip site financially backed by Time Warner, had a web of tipsters and informants, and cared little about the celebrities they lambasted. *TMZ* took the chapters-in-a-saga method of gossip publishing developed by *Confidential* and updated it for the online world. *TMZ* employed videographers that could be in celebrity hotspots for hours, and published any new information they had about a story every day. Janice Min, editor-in-chief of *US Weekly* from 2002 to 2009, complained to the *New York Times* about how difficult it was to compete with *TMZ*, but she acknowledged: "It's great to have them out there. It's like going to an all-you-can-eat buffet where you never get full."[2]

With blogs siphoning off their viewership and stealing their content, the weeklies played dirty. A single photo could generate thousands of magazine sales, so weeklies fought in bitter, intense bidding wars. *People* spent $75,000 for a photo of Jennifer Lopez reading *Us Weekly* simply to prevent *Us* from publishing it. Photo agencies sprung up, which facilitated the creation, sale, and consumption of paparazzi photos by acting as middlemen between the photographers and the tabloids. Agencies like X17 and Bauer-Griffin paid their guerrilla photographers steady salaries to stalk celebs, then squeezed money out of their pictures by selling them to websites, magazines, and TV programs in addition to the standard weeklies.

The tabloid industry's promise of high pay attracted a new wave of paparazzi. Groups of photographers launched complicated maneuvers that cornered a celebrity into producing a good photo. The paps could surveil stars twenty-four hours a day, hiding in garbage cans, and sometimes soaring above their targets in rented helicopters. By 2005, *Us* got up to 50,000 images every week, 75 percent of them from paparazzi. As the paparazzi industry had become bigger and more profitable than ever, photographers were primed to stalk a celebrity's moves night and day.

Britney was their cash cow. Armed with digital cameras that could take thousands of photos in quick succession, a squadron of paparazzi desperate for cash, and websites that could provide celebrity updates 24/7, tabloids could wring Britney for all she was worth. In 2007, images of Britney made photo agency X17 $3 million. Up to forty-five X17 paps shot Britney every night. The combined value of Britney shots, according to *Vanity Fair*, exceeded $100 million a year, and helped make Britney Spears the most popular search term on *Yahoo* in 2007, as it had been for six of the past seven years. As Harvey Levin, the founder of *TMZ*, put it in 2006: "Britney is gold. She is crack to our readers. Her life is a complete trainwreck, and I thank God for her every day."

In keeping with these changes to the gossip industry, *Blackout* depicts celebrity culture as a nightmare of constant surveillance. On "Piece of Me" she talks about getting groceries and sneaking away for a furtive vacation but never able to find peace; the cameras still follow her. The chorus takes the form of a barrage of headlines, not unlike the pop-ups on a gossip blog or the line of titles across the newsstand. Throughout the record, there will be a casual mention of the people who are interested in watching her, an unnamed "they" who want to gawk at her in the club or take her photo or gossip about her paramours. Like in her life under the aughts celebrity panopticon, an audience is always subtly present in *Blackout*.

Blackout also draws attention to the tabloids' contradictory barrage of takedowns and praise. By the time of *Blackout*'s recording, the 2000s gossip machine had been well oiled. Tabloids dump seemingly unrelated updates constantly— Britney has a meltdown in a shoot for *OK! Magazine*, Britney goes commando on her way to the club, Britney drops her kid—and lets the reader put together the larger narrative. "Piece of Me" explores this fragmentary storytelling style most acutely. The tabloids prop her up for being rich and famous, embodying the American dream, but then tear her down for wearing a revealing outfit on the way to the grocery store or for being a mom and a working woman. She's somehow too fat and too thin. "You want a piece of me" could be a statement of fact as well as a question. By 2007, Britney no longer had a coherent public image—she had been pummeled into pieces, scattered across different photos and articles and websites.

The mainstream media's dogged, ubiquitous Britney coverage has roots in structural changes to the entertainment industry. In 2007, it seemed that every news outlet trafficked in celebrity gossip. Even if you avoided tabloid drama out of principle, or dismissed Britney for being a hooligan or a floozy, you couldn't escape her. This was a result of a series of conglomerations in the late 1980 and mid-1990s, where large entertainment companies like Time and Warner, Sony and Columbia, Viacom and Paramount joined forces. As these companies ballooned, they sought out smaller titles that could cross-promote their projects. Gossip outlets—with a demographic squarely in the 18–34-year-old market—could provide cheap, quick promotion. So large media conglomerates financed the very magazines that criticized them, since all press, apparently, was good press.

As such, mainstream news channels covered Britney's demise with the same attention as serious political news. In 1992, *Entertainment Weekly*, in partnership with the E! entertainment channel, distributed shortened versions of "Entertainment Weekly's News Report" to HBO and CBS radio networks. Then Time Warner sold its stake in E! to Disney and Comcast. Disney had just acquired ABC, and CEO Michael Eisner saw E! as a property that provided an opportunity for cross-promotion, where ABC could air specials that redirected viewers to E! and Disney and vice versa. Similarly, in 1995, when Time Warner merged with Turner, which included CNN, CNN would use content from *Entertainment Weekly* as part of its "Newsstand" program, a deep-dive show that aired three times a week. In 2001, Disney bought a 50 percent stake in *Us Weekly*, the most tame of the tabloids and a "nonaggressive, celebrity-friendly, synergy-ready" product, according to the *New York Times*. Within months of the agreement, ABC News began feeding a ninety-second "*Us* Report" to ABC affiliates, and *Us*-branded segments popped up on "The View" and "Good Morning America."

As "real news" outlets began advertising and promoting "news to amuse," pundits began to worry. Why was CNN dabbling in softball celebrity content? The nonstop coverage of Britney's antics in the mid-2000s seemed particularly inane when sandwiched between dispiriting updates about the United States's entrance into war. Celebrity content and geopolitical news occupied the same stage, and the two grew increasingly difficult to distinguish from each other in the *way* they were broadcasted. In 2008, Harvey Levin, founder of *TMZ*, told *Rolling Stone*, "We serialize Britney Spears. She's our President Bush."[3] Meanwhile, Sheeraz Hasan, who founded *hollywood.tv*, told the same publication: "Everything Britney does is news—Britney pumps gas, Britney forgets to put milk in her coffee—and there's a war going on, man!"[4] Britney seemed like such a distraction from America's geopolitical failures that a conspiracy theory arose, suggesting that Bush purposefully triggered Britney's meltdowns to distract from his own failures. Both hard and soft news outlets had train wrecks to follow: *TMZ* had Britney, CNN had George W. Bush. It was bad enough that America was at war, but it was even worse that the public couldn't be bothered to care. Instead, they turned their attention to pretty blonde women and who they were sleeping with, how much they drank, whether they wore underwear on their way to the club. Britney became a sign that Americans were just as vapid and uninformed as the celebrities they obsessed over. This seemed to elevate Britney to levels of gravity and importance she didn't seem to deserve.

Britney's fame was a self-fulfilling prophecy. The paparazzi followed her because the tabloids spent big on Britney photos; the tabloids snapped up Britney photos because people continued to find her fascinating; people lapped up Britney updates because she was on every channel, on every magazine cover. You couldn't ignore her, and it wasn't really clear *why*.

But *Blackout* offers a precise account of why Britney held people's attention. The songs on the album that most explicitly explore how Britney captivates the public— "Freakshow," "Gimme More," "Toy Soldier," "Piece of Me"— all focus on sex. In all of these songs Britney is grinding in the club with a new lover, while an ambiguous crowd of voyeurs and photographers look on. On "Toy Soldier" we hear a few people gossip about Britney, marveling about how "every man is wanting" her. she doesn't get off on seeing her sex life become a spectator sport; it's just a fact of her life. "We can get down like there's no one around, but they keep watching," she says on "Gimme More."

This preoccupation with Britney's sex life on *Blackout* reflects a moral panic she embodied about how young white girls had sex. Throughout the early aughts there seemed to be an explosion of sexual behavior that was once considered "trashy" among the white-middle class. Busty, scantily-clad models posed, mid-striptease on the covers of "lad mags" like *Esquire* and *GQ* and women's weeklies like *Cosmo* and *Glamour*. It wasn't just the centerfolds. In reality show "Girls Gone Wild," college girls on spring break stripped and made out on national television. Enough women bought Jenna Jamison's *How to Make Love Like a Porn Star* that it made the bestseller list. Reading *Playboy* or getting a Brazilian wax seemed less like pandering to the male gaze and more like owning one's sexuality. Landing a corporate job and participating in a wet T-Shirt contest, say, no longer appeared to be mutually exclusive. Being a hot blonde had suddenly become transgressive, but not so transgressive that it'd upset her parents. It was the sexual revolution for popular kids.

Britney slotted into this milieu perfectly. Britney seemed like a perfect sex object, a virgin in a latex bodysuit. She saw no contradiction between being a sweet, Christian girl-next-door and a sexy video vixen. In her first music video, the infamous "...Baby One More Time," she pranced around a high school in a skimpy schoolgirl skirt, but maintained that it had no bearing on her actual sex life—she was a virgin. This "contradiction" vexed the press and the public alike. While Britney maintained that she hadn't yet had sex, various paramours like Justin Timberlake and Fred Durst couldn't resist revealing that they had slept with the Princess of Pop, provoking a fruitless and vacuous investigation into Britney's virginity. But regardless of whether she was or was not having sex, Britney's public persona depended on juxtaposing these seemingly irreconcilable states of girlish purity and risqué maturity. She was the ideal of raunch culture; she was sexy in a way that supplemented her ambition and didn't conflict with her innocence.

Britney wasn't the only poster girl for raunch culture; Lindsay Lohan and Paris Hilton also seesawed between Disney-channel piety and fun-loving skankiness. It's telling that all of them are white—only white women could pull off that kind of balancing act. Mainstream society objectifies girls of color, particularly Black girls, well before puberty. They have to fight to be seen as innocent. Though raunch culture assures that the door is always left open for white women to return to prim and proper respectability after a "slutty" phase, this promise does not hold true for women of color.

As such, the most explosive criticisms of Britney's sexuality ventriloquized pearl-clutching white parents. After all, the target demographic for Britney's music—alongside the output of her raunchy counterparts, Lindsay Lohan and Paris Hilton—was assumed to be tweens and teens. Britney, Paris, and Lindsay became the "Brit Pack," a troublemaking trio that, through their carefree, fun-loving attitudes, enticed young women into a life of drinking, drugs, and casual sex. It didn't seem to matter that the three girls were mere acquaintances. Paris and Britney went clubbing together, but their relationship didn't seem especially close. Lindsay and Paris's friendship went up in flames when Lindsay started going out with Paris's ex. They've been bitterly feuding ever since. Britney and Lindsay had no relationship to speak of. Nevertheless, fearful parents treated the Brit Pack as a united front determined to destroy their daughters. A poll conducted by *Newsweek* in 2007 suggested that 77 percent of Americans believed that the Brit Pack had too much influence on young girls. It was as if her outbursts and overdoses were Britney's penance for being too sexy, too soon, and their daughters could be headed in the same direction.

As a result, ragging on Britney Spears took on a moral intensity. Diane Sawyer infamously told Britney in 2003 that she "upset a lot of mothers in this country," because of her risqué outfits.[5] The first lady of Maryland at the time, Kendel Ehrlich, spoke at a domestic violence conference and announced that same year, "You know, really, if I had the opportunity to shoot Britney Spears, I think I would." A headline ran in the *Los Angeles Times* in 2003: "It's All the Rage Now: Hating Britney Spears."[6] The more Britney appeared in the public eye, disheveled and angry and scantily clad, the more people hated her; the more people hated her, the more profitable her photos became, making her an even more attractive target for the paparazzi.

To hate Britney for her sexualization by the media—which was, for the most part, exploitative and out of her control—seems unfair. But blaming Britney reflected the lack of nuance in conversations about raunch culture, and around female sexuality more broadly. The rise of raunch could not get off the ground without women's enthusiastic consent, or at least the illusion of it. *Girls Gone Wild*, one of the clearest depictions of this sexual ethos, staged scenes of consent where girls maintain that they're thrilled to shed their clothes for the camera. As Karen C. Pitcher notes in "The Staging of Agency in Girls Gone Wild," most scenes of a *GGW* video include a consent process on camera, in which the girls claim to be over eighteen and excited to participate, even if they were too drunk to remember they'd done it the next morning. Pandering to the male gaze could become transgressive and even feminist, precisely because women eagerly chose to take part.

In its aggressive staging of consent, *GGW* invoked a false dichotomy that haunted the sexual discourse: many women felt that they had either present themselves as sexual agents or victims of patriarchy in order for their sexuality to be legible. Many women, understandably, chose to present themselves as empowered and in control. But this framing conceals the nuances of sexual exploitation that extend beyond consent. A girl gone wild can choose to flash the camera and note that she did so because she was drunk, or because the cameraman told her it wasn't a big deal, or simply because she thought it'd be fun. She could even feel all of these things at the same time, pulling her in different directions. It seems unfair to impose a binary—she either *chose* to strip, or was *forced* to strip—onto this situation. In reality, "raunch culture" was neither inherently oppressive nor inherently empowering. It depended on why a woman chose to participate, whether someone was twisting her arm.

Looked at with a more nuanced lens, Britney's relationship with her sexuality seemed less naive than her conservative critics thought. For the infamous ". . .Baby One More Time" music video, the director, seeming to anticipate rumors that he forced the teenage Britney to act sexy, wrote on the FAQ section of his website: "I wrote an idea which sucked, so the label put me back on the phone with Britney who told me she wanted to make a video where she was stuck in a classroom thinking about boys and we took it from there."[7] It seemed that in this situation, with a director willing to cater to her vision, Britney wearing a skimpy outfit was a way for her to flaunt her nascent sexual power. "All I did was tie up my shirt!" she said to *Rolling Stone* in 1999.[8] "I'm wearing a sports bra under it. Sure, I'm wearing thigh-highs, but kids wear those—it's the style. Have you seen MTV—all those girls in thongs?"[9]

For that same article quoted above, David LaChapelle shot Britney for the cover of *Rolling Stone*. The image showed a sultry Spears in her childhood bedroom, laying on pink satin sheets, with her sweater unbuttoned to reveal a bra and pink polka-dot boy-shorts. She clutches a purple stuffed Teletubby in one hand, but looks into the camera with her lips slightly parted. "Into the heart, mind, and bedroom of a teen dream," the cover enticed. In this iconic image, childishness and sensuality collided, making explicit the pedophilic undertones sublimated in her star persona. When she talked about the photo, she said she didn't know what she was getting into. In an interview later in her career, in 2003, she was asked how she knew she had become a sex symbol, as if, like aging or puberty, her sexuality was something she must reckon with rather than control. She answered:

> How did I realize [I was a sex symbol]? Probably the first *Rolling Stone* cover by David LaChapelle. He came in and did the photos and totally tricked me. They were really cool but I didn't really know what the hell I was doing. And, to be totally honest with you, at the time I was sixteen, so I really didn't. I was back in my bedroom, and I had my little sweater on and he was like, "Undo your sweater a little bit more." The whole thing was about me being into dolls, and in my naïve mind I was like, "Here are my dolls!" and now I look back and I'm like, "Oh my gosh, what the hell?" But he did a very good job of portraying me in that way. It certainly wasn't peaches and cream.

She felt ambivalent, as if the photographers were taking something from her that she didn't know she had.

In a similar sense, the public didn't seem to grasp that Britney was not always willing to be photographed, in a way that mirrored her conservative critics' inability to understand that her willingness to flaunt her body depended on the situation. If Britney was depressed or frightened by the constant attention, the tabloids seemed not to know it. To them, she was actively involved in constructing her image. "Forever, she has been in on the joke," said Harvey Levin of *TMZ*.[10] Rumor had it that Britney stayed up late reading gossip blogs, and X17's photographers maintain that she frequently left comments on their posts, and sometimes even called them up to restage unflattering shots. Meg Handler, a writer for *Star Magazine*, told the *Atlantic*: "Those photographers were called. Most of the time, her people called. 'Britney's going to be here.' 'Britney's going to be there.' That's how it worked.'"[11] The paps in *Paparazzi: Full Throttle* seem to view their relationship as mutually beneficial. Paparazzo Jose even looks straight into the camera and thanks her for being one of the nicest celebrities in the business. In the parking lot of a mall, she waves at the paparazzi and flashes a smile, saying "I love you guys. Party at my house." How could she smile for the pictures in one moment and declare herself a victim in the next?

It's crucial to note that many of these accounts of Britney's supposed love of the paparazzi didn't come from Britney herself. The paparazzi observed her from a distance and perhaps mistook her sweet Southern-girl politeness for genuine appreciation. The source of much of the above information came from Sam Lutfi, a shady figure who served as Britney's unofficial manager for much of 2007 and

2008. A lot is unclear about Sam's relationship to Britney. What we do know has been filtered through the accounts of Britney's father, Jamie, who felt that Lutfi was using Britney's instability to rob her blind. That said, it's hard to imagine that Lutfi had intentions more malevolent than Jamie, who, by most accounts, has been willing to throw Britney under the bus whenever possible to secure a larger slice of her vast fortune. But I wouldn't call Sam a good influence—rumor has it that Sam would drug Britney by hiding pills in her food. He certainly worked in cahoots with the paps, tipping agencies like X17 to let them know where Britney would be.

Sometimes Britney smiled and posed for the cameras, sometimes she cussed them out. Either way, her handlers called the press and herded her into the crowd to get her photo taken, over and over again. It seemed irrelevant whether this was something she wanted. Besides, focusing on the paparazzi rather than the larger ecosystem that profited off of her surveillance obscures the true forces that fueled her exploitation. Mainstream media used Los Angeles's paparazzi, who were overwhelmingly Latine, and often recent immigrants, as scapegoats for the excesses of aughts celebrity culture. Celebrities and commentators have used racist metaphors to describe them as "pack animals," "pests," and "vermin," while anti-paparazzi laws implemented in the early 2010s have criminalized the profession. The tabloids and news outlets who profited most off of these images skirted the blame, even though they stoked the outrage that made Britney such an attractive target to begin with.

The ambiguities of consent surrounding Britney's sexuality and her willingness to be photographed laid bare the exploitation latent in the pressures of 2000's raunch and tabloid culture. Beauty, sensuality, and attention are all forms of power, and both raunch and celebrity promised that women could claim this power without repercussions. But this kind of empowerment is fleeting and could easily warp into something sinister. Though sexual power and celebrity masquerade as privilege, they cannot be codified into structural advantage, just as winning the lottery doesn't imbue the vast advantages of generational wealth. Instead, the young woman's sexual power gets proffered and manipulated and sold by whoever's shrewd enough to profit off it.

We see it over and over again. I think of the girls who went wild, who would never have considered stripping until a cameraman stopped to ask. I think of the interviewer asking Britney when she knew that she had become a sex symbol, implying that her objectification was somehow inevitable, or had been decided by forces out of her control. In all these cases, a young woman can only claim sexual power when someone else sees her that way. A sexy teen is a perfect object in a media landscape that panders to male tastes—she has the body of a woman without knowing what it's worth; she can't feel beautiful until someone tells her so. In this fantasy, those who objectify her bestow her with power and set its limits. They decide when the famous young woman inevitably ceases to be young and beautiful, while the tabloids lay in wait to sell photos of her downfall. In any case, someone profits.

On "Piece of Me" Britney manages to escape this dynamic. She's neither a victim nor the one in control. Instead, she's evasive. The identities she dons, from "Miss American

Dream" and "Mrs. Lifestyles of the Rich and Famous" to "Miss Bad Media Karma" and "Mrs. 'Most likely to get on TV for strippin' on the streets,'" are a form of armor. Though everyone may want a piece of her, that's all that they can get.

***

In the 2007 movie "Music and Lyrics," a charming, if slight, rom-com starring Hugh Grant and Drew Barrymore, the antagonist of the film is a blonde sexpot pop singer named Cora. She's introduced on the set of a music video, sauntering around a faux-Buddhist monastery in a green sequined bikini, shaking her hips to a song called "Buddha's Delight." The song's purportedly about her deep connection to Buddhism, but watching the video, it seems more likely an excuse to show off her svelte physique and stare down the camera with her heavy-lidded bedroom eyes.

The character clearly represents the vapidity of mainstream pop, evoking any number of blonde chanteuses from Shakira to Christina Aguilera. But Cora seems to be a stand-in for one pop star in particular. The song she performs, "Buddha's Delight," blends a high-BPM drum track and sampled Middle Eastern synth hook with a choppy, artificial-sounding acoustic guitar, before breaking into a surf-rock groove. On the pre-chorus, Cora sings in airy falsetto and then belts the last part of the chorus. This song sounds suspiciously familiar; everything from the song's structure to its idiosyncratic details were ripped almost exactly from Britney's hit song "Toxic." This is no accident. After all, both songs, the parody Britney and actual Britney, were written by the same songwriting duo: Swedish producers Bloodshy and Avant.

Bloodshy and Avant were key Britney collaborators, particularly on *Blackout*—they wrote almost as many songs on the album as Danja did. Yet they rarely claim ownership over the record, and have given only a handful of interviews throughout their careers. Though their work has been consistently innovative and successful, they don't seem to see themselves as producer-auteurs like Timbaland or Max Martin, and they seem to shun the public eye. For producers so uninterested in fame, it seems strange that they were able to pen "Piece of Me."

Christian Karlsson and Pontus Winnberg, aka "Bloodshy and Avant" grew up in Gothenburg, Sweden. They approached pop music from opposite perspectives. Winnberg (Avant), a piano prodigy, learned music theory from his dad, a classical music professor. Meanwhile, Karlsson (Bloodshy), passed the time skateboarding, occasionally dabbling in hip-hop production. They crossed paths when Karlsson was in Goldmine, a Swedish hip-hop group, and Winnberg was in another band. American labels discovered Goldmine and scooped up Karlsson to work with Neneh Cherry and Jay-Z. As he got more and more offers, Karlsson couldn't keep up with all the work, so he called up Winnberg to see if he wanted to work together.

Their first success was Christina Milian's "AM to PM." It's uncanny how immediately they established their signature style: drastically altering the tone of the song throughout, juxtaposing musical modes that shouldn't necessarily fit together. The song begins with a kick-y beat with a warbling synth underneath. The choppiness of the beat allows for a lot of negative space and pauses in between chord hits. Right when you get used to this aggressive, off-kilter beat, everything drops out save for a graceful harp riff, some wet snares, and snaps. Then, after the third chorus, the song shifts again. The bridge brings in arpeggios of warped video game synths, with no drums whatsoever. Milian's label, Murder Inc. Records, was unsure about the song. They said that the song's subject matter, a club night, was too risqué, because, according to Karlsson, these songs are played at the club rather than on the radio, which generates less revenue.

Much to the label's surprise, the song ended up a minor hit, charting at number twenty-seven in the US Hot 100. Studio execs called Karlsson and Winnberg to replicate it for more famous artists. In a seven-day sprint with fellow songwriter Cathy Dennis, they crafted a song called "Toxic" intended for Janet Jackson, including all the things that made "AM to PM" a hit: the wild string sample, the high BPM, the constant shifts in tone and musical tradition. Dennis ended up pitching the song to Kylie Minogue, who passed. "Toxic" stayed in the vault until Karlsson and Winnberg were invited to work with Britney on *In the Zone*. After they showed Britney's team what they had, the label asked for more. Karlsson and Winberg mentioned that they had another song in the drawer—"Toxic." They played it, and her team went silent, before disappearing into another room. After a few minutes, they returned to the studio. The verdict: they wanted it.

Britney's reps didn't think it was single-worthy, and Karlsson and Winnberg knew it. The label gave them the same note they always got: their work sounded too strange for the Top 40. Karlsson and Winnberg had no idea if they ended up putting "Toxic" on *In the Zone*, or nixing it altogether. But the track made the album, and once it was released, listeners were downloading "Toxic" on iTunes much more than any song on *In the Zone*, even the singles. Britney's A&R called the duo and said the song could be a dark horse. When they released "Toxic" as a single, it topped pop charts around the world.

Through "Toxic," Karlsson and Winnberg entered Britney's inner circle. She even brought them with her to tour in Europe. There, Bloodshy and Avant were shocked to find how difficult it was for Britney to navigate the world normally. When they had coffee in the hotel courtyard, their guards had to hang makeshift drapes so no one could spot them. Even then, the paparazzi hung from trees, shouting provocations. When they got to Hamburg, Britney whispered to Karlsson and Winnberg that they should ditch the guards and go out on the town. They slipped out down a back road, but someone saw them and started chasing them down. As they ran, the crowd continued to grow, until at least a hundred people were tailing them. They fled into a jewelry store, but the crowd tried to force their way in, and the owner panicked and kicked them out. They managed to escape into a taxi and head to the Reeperbahn, a famous Hamburg club, but the experience scared them.

In the years following *In the Zone*, Karlsson and Winnberg remained fiercely loyal to Britney. Before *Blackout*, Bloodshy and Avant penned songs for her short-lived MTV reality show, Britney + Kevin: Chaotic, as well as the theme song to her little sister's Nickelodeon show, *Zoey 101*. They seemed more invested in Britney's well-being and her relationships with her tabloid dramas than any of her other producers. After Justin Timberlake released his infamous song "Cry Me a River," which capitalized on the rumors surrounding his relationship with Britney, Winnberg and Karlsson thought she should respond with a song of her own. Along with "Toxic" co-writer Cathy Dennis, they crafted the song "Sweet Dreams My LA Ex." The chorus accuses: "Can't you stop playing that record again? Find somebody else to talk about." They pitched it to Britney, but her team insisted that she couldn't sing about her personal life. They gave it to a British pop star, Rachel Stevens, instead, and the song peaked at number two on the British charts. After *Blackout*, they produced a number of hits on almost all of her subsequent albums, from *My Prerogative* to *Femme Fatale*.

When Karlsson and Winnberg were inevitably brought on to *Blackout*, they played by the rules. The songs that made the cut meander less than their early work. Their music for *Blackout* sticks to a central groove and purely electronic sounds rather than mixing and matching acoustic guitars and samples. In their early work, you can hear glitchy synths gurgling in the background, but on *Blackout* they brought them to the foreground. On "Toy Soldier," and "Freakshow," unstable layers of synths create lurching beats.

After a month or so of working on *Blackout*, they had finished their tracks for the album, but Britney's A&R wanted them to write just one more song. This was their last week in Los Angeles, and they had burned out. They brought in fellow Swede Klas Åhlund to do the lyrics, and spent the week slacking off and ordering food to the studio. The dramas of her personal life meant that Britney couldn't write with them, or spend twenty hours in the studio at a time like she did in the old days. After procrastinating for a while, they had only three days left to write a song, and Karlsson and Winnberg started reflecting on their experience in Hamburg. Karlsson and Winnberg thought this experience was good material. So they decided to do what they did best: break the rules.

The resulting song, "Piece of Me," plumbed not only their experiences with Britney, but their own complicated feelings about modern pop. Throughout their career, Bloodshy & Avant have expressed disgust with the hit-making process. In 2016, they turned down writing for Beyoncé and Madonna to start their own band, Miike Snow, with American singer Andrew Wyatt. Their goal was to create an anti-band, with no real front man, no personas, and no theatrics. "Our goal is that the songs are just so good—so hooky, and with so much tension and release—that you don't care if the singer is wearing a certain fashion designer," Wyatt said in a profile of the band in the *Los Angeles Times*. "That's not what your investment is."[12]

"Piece of Me" expressed Winnberg and Karlsson's weariness with the industry. The song didn't feel like an emotional statement about the traumas of fame because it wasn't one. After years of being told what they could and couldn't write, Karlsson and Winnberg were tired of making hits. They wrote from the perspective of a Britney not unlike themselves: the Britney of "Piece of Me," takes a systemic view of celebrity culture, bemoaning its ability to transform a chore into a headline. "No wonder there's panic in the industry," she scoffs on the song, "I mean, *please*."[13] She may not have articulated these sentiments in her own words on "Piece of Me," but Karlsson and Winnberg had known her long enough to have a sense of how she felt. After all, they had helped her produce and record "Mona Lisa," the song she had written in 2004 about the horrors of fame. Karlsson and Winnberg imbued "Piece of Me" with "Mona Lisa's" jadedness and discontent, informing the song with her perspective even when she couldn't speak for herself.

"Piece of Me" was the most critically acclaimed track on *Blackout*. Rob Sheffield, who reviewed the album for *Rolling Stone* on release, wrote in 2017 that "'Piece of Me' is the peak of the album—and maybe Britney's career."[14] It seemed to speak to critics in their language: the pundit class may have viewed Britney as a representation of pop culture's superficiality, but "Piece of Me" showed that Britney could be self-aware enough to criticize her industry.

Bloodshy and Avant produced three other songs on *Blackout*, all of which also explore the effects of fame. On "Freakshow," and "Radar" Britney is trying to get with someone on the dance floor, but is surrounded by people watching them; on the bridge for "Toy Soldier," a few imagined club-goers spread rumors about Britney's promiscuity. Even on songs where she seems to lose herself dancing in the darkness, Britney never finds privacy. There's always a "camera flashing" nearby or someone leering, looking for a "peep-show." Though *Blackout* is an album of club bangers, its subject—more than fucking or dancing or drinking—is the difficulty of establishing a self in the public eye. Sometimes she gets off on the attention, like in "Gimme

More"; sometimes she gets annoyed with it, like on "Break the Ice." The record feels no need to resolve those inconsistencies. Britney never finds peace, never splits herself into her public and private selves. This ambiguity reflects Britney's lack of control. In her real life, it didn't matter whether she wanted the attention or not; the paparazzi continued to show up and the headlines kept coming. "Piece of Me," and *Blackout*, redirected public discourse away from Britney herself and back towards the celebrity industry as a whole.

It's hard to know if Britney actually had such a detached, intellectualized perspective. This bored, jaded attitude would be hard to maintain given all that she went through, from losing custody over her kids to her frequent hospitalizations. But Britney clearly identified with the perspective of the song. It turned out to be one of the few Bloodshy & Avant tracks that they didn't have to argue their way onto the album. Britney immediately connected to the song. After they sent her "Piece of Me," she went straight to the car to memorize the lyrics. When she arrived at the studio the next day, she had already listened to "Piece of Me" so many times that she managed to record her vocals in just a half-hour. In the booth, she was able to be "Ms. You Want a Piece of Me" even if she had to return into the public eye after she left.

*   *   *

In 2006, Britney went out with Paris Hilton, only to be joined in her car by Lindsay Lohan. This was the first time the public saw the Brit Pack in the same place. A picture of this tableaux, titled "Bimbo Summit," ran on the cover of the *New York Post*, with the three starlets smiling conspiratorially like a few high school girls on their way to prom. Together, they were never more powerful. These women, it seemed, could send the world into a tizzy just by spreading their legs. The *Post* called them the "three bimbos of the apocalypse."

This apocalypse never came. Like so many tabloid darlings before them, the Brit Pack crashed and burned. In 2006, Paris got a DUI, went to jail, and faded from the public eye. In 2008, Britney was legally stripped of her freedom via a conservatorship that put her father in control of all aspects of her life, from what kind of music she could record to what she could buy at Starbucks. Lindsay, banned permanently from the Chateau Marmont, fled to Mykonos, then to Dubai. By 2012, the summit was over, and the bimbos had fallen back down to ground level.

It seemed that the sexual freedom the bimbos represented faded away, too. The siren song of raunch culture promised that you no longer had to choose between being a Madonna or a whore: you could be a sweet college girl-next-door and still go wild for the night. But that, too, was a scam. The patriarchal media exploited the bimbos, the tabloids profited off them, the conservatives made them out to be whores and devils, and the second-wave feminists lambasted them for seeming to enjoy their own oppression.

In retrospect, we no longer see Britney as the vacant, "famous for being famous" slut that embodied America's cultural decline. Instead, we blame the toxicity of the early aughts on the pundits and shock jocks and paparazzi that harassed her. A *New York Times* documentary about Britney came out in February 2021, which argued that Britney was a victim rather than a villain. In the documentarians' hands, Britney's rise to fame incurred endless invasions of her privacy, starting at the age of sixteen and lasting well into her thirties. This narrative was so affecting that many of Britney's most zealous stalkers, from Perez Hilton to *TMZ*, have apologized to her for what they had done.

Lindsay Lohan has not quite had the same image rehabilitation as Britney. She tried to snag indie cred with a starring role in Bret Easton Ellis and Paul Schrader's prestige drama *The Canyons*, alongside porn star James Deen. But the movie flopped—and working with her seemed more difficult than ever. A. O. Scott reported for the *New York Times* about the drama she caused on set, in a cruel article headlined "This Is What Happens When You Cast Lindsay Lohan in a Movie." She had a short-lived reality TV show about her beachside club in Mykonos, before it folded. Still, after the Britney documentary, a 2013 interview with David Letterman and Lindsay Lohan resurfaced on Twitter, where he presses her about her upcoming trip to rehab. The exchange was seen as banal at the time. Though she cried in the interview, the press dismissed the theatrics as business as usual: an article in the *Los Angeles Times* said "When Lindsay Lohan cries, it often has something to do with court" and a *Newsday* recap similarly quipped: "It was the usual, or deja vu all over again."[15] But when someone posted the video on Twitter in February 2021, the conversation changed completely: "this . . . is horrifying to watch now," the poster wrote.[16]

Unlike Britney or Lindsay, Paris has successfully cast her persona in a more flattering light, on her own terms. Paris commissioned a documentary that juxtaposes her moments in the spotlight, winking at the press and saying "that's hot" in her signature valley-girl drawl, with her "real" self, who's guarded and down-to-earth, puttering around her perpetually messy house in a ratty pair of sweatpants. She wasn't always a Barbie come to life. As a teen, she was smart and withdrawn, with aims to be a veterinarian. Her classmates remember her always raising her hand; behind the valley-girl facade, she's "actually brilliant," as her mother put it. But, according to the documentary, a single experience changed her from a sweet, precocious child into the glitzy reality star she would eventually become. As a teenager, she started sneaking out of her Upper East Side penthouse to go clubbing downtown, shedding the pressures of well-heeled debutante life. Her parents weren't pleased about this development. Worried about their "troubled teen," they had her kidnapped and sent away to a reform school in Provo, Utah. There, she was tortured and starved and even placed in solitary confinement. She decided, crumpled into a ball on the floor of her cell, that she would recede behind a persona that could protect her.

Perhaps this narrative is an honest reflection of how Paris understands her past. The experience of being stolen from one's house and imprisoned at such a young age is a nightmare come true, one that could irrevocably change the course of a girl's life. Regardless, this film makes a remarkably conservative argument, that Paris's superficial "bimbo" act was not *really* Paris, but rather a product of her trauma. Though the film wants us to take Paris seriously, it amputates her vapid persona and contrasts it with her true "interior" self, who's smart, self-aware, and unimpressed by ritzy pleasures like gowns and designer bags. The end of the documentary provides some acknowledgment that Paris's bimbo persona may not entirely be a shield or a facade, and that, alternately, "authenticity" can be a canny way to rebrand. In the last scene of the film, a voice from behind the camera asks her, looking out from her balcony into the Los Angeles basin, whether she will finally let go of her brand. Paris smirks. "No," she says.

Lurking behind this narrative is a more pointed story about the suffocating effects of girlhood, a story that begins well before Paris was born. Paris's mother Kathy had been in showbiz since she was a diaper model. Kathy's childhood was steeped in Hollywood debauchery, as her mother ogled high-rollers over vodka tonics at the Polo Lounge and shoved Kathy and her sisters into child stardom to keep the cash flowing. Kathy envisioned a safer childhood for Paris, with debutante balls and cotillions, prep schools and seven-course dinners. Kathy kept Paris on a tight leash: no boys, no parties, no late nights. Paris, like most teens, rebelled. So Kathy sent her to Provo, where the penalties for acting out were catastrophic.

But Paris didn't back down. Instead, she decided to become her parents' worst nightmare: a dolt, a shopaholic, a slut. If she couldn't be herself, she might as well be someone more fun. She could embody a character so impenetrable that no one could touch her. The tabloids could call her stupid or selfish and it wouldn't matter. They were up in arms about a work of fiction.

What was so compelling and taboo about Britney and Paris and the rest of the bimbos was that they fabulated personalities so subversive and opaque that it seemed like nothing could break them. They wore their femininity like drag, taking the most pathetic, ugly qualities associated with women—promiscuity, idiocy, blind consumerism—and shoving them down your throat. Call the bimbo dumb, call her a menace or a whore or a bad influence. Who cares? You can get away with a lot when people aren't taking you seriously.

Now I know that Paris's persona did not protect her. It made her famous, it raked in cash, it became the face of an empire of reality shows and perfumes and clothing lines. But after years of taking photos with fans and going to galas, Paris realized that her persona had become its own kind of constraint, with its own pressures. It didn't matter whether she was a party girl or a debutante—she was still just a facade, afraid to probe underneath. The take-no-prisoners Britney on *Blackout* was an act, too, a persona formulated by a couple of producers.

But the apocalypse the *New York Post* feared is still alive on *Blackout*. Regardless of who wrote the songs, *Blackout* creates a narrative in which Britney can see the chaos of her life in more positive terms. As Britney sings about dancing and drinking and flirting, synths growl and stutter as if the walls were crumbling around her. Even in the darkness of the club she's still in the spotlight; the paparazzi are never far behind. But she doesn't seem to care. She's out of control, and so is everything else. It sounds like fun.

Notes

1   Grigoriadis, Vanessa. "The Tragedy of Britney Spears." *Rolling Stone* (blog), February 21, 2008. https://www.rollingstone.com/feature/the-tragedy-of-britney-spears-2-254735/.

2 Weiner, Allison Hope. "The Web Site Celebrities Fear." *The New York Times*, June 25, 2007. https://www.nytimes.com/2007/06/25/business/media/25tmz.html.

3 Grigoriadis, "The Tragedy of Britney Spears."

4 Ibid.

5 Willen, Claudia. "Fans Are Calling for Diane Sawyer to Apologize to Britney Spears after a 'disgusting' 2003 Interview Was Included in a New Documentary." *Insider*, February 9, 2021. https://www.insider.com/britney-spears-diane-sawyer-2003-interview-fan-backlash-documentary-reactions-2021-2.

6 Stepp, Laura Sessions. "It's All the Rage Now: Hating Britney Spears." *Los Angeles Times*, November 28, 2003. https://www.latimes.com/archives/la-xpm-2003-nov-28-et-stepp28-story.html.

7 Nigel Dick - Director. "Details of … Britney Videos." n.d. https://www.nigeldick.com/about-dick/dick-fuq/details-of-britney-videos/.

8 Daly, Steven. "Britney Spears, Teen Queen: Rolling Stone's 1999 Cover Story." *Rolling Stone* (blog), March 29, 2011. https://www.rollingstone.com/music/music-news/britney-spears-teen-queen-rolling-stones-1999-cover-story-254871/.

9 Ibid.

10 Samuels, David. "Shooting Britney." *The Atlantic*, April 2008. https://www.theatlantic.com/magazine/archive/2008/04/shooting-britney/306735/.

11 Ibid.

12 Wood, Mikael. "The Men of Miike Snow Make Pop Music—But They're Not Pop Stars." *Los Angeles Times*, March 10,

2016. https://www.latimes.com/entertainment/music/posts/la-et-ms-miike-snow-iii-interview-20160310-story.html.

13 Spears, Britney. *Piece of Me*. Jive Records, November 27, 2007.

14 Sheffield, Rob. "Britney Spears' Blackout: Punk Masterpiece." *Rolling Stone*, October 30, 2017. https://www.rollingstone.com/music/music-news/britney-spears-blackout-a-salute-to-her-misunderstood-punk-masterpiece-121525/.

15 D'Zurilla, Christie. "Lindsay Lohan Cries on David Letterman's Show." *Los Angeles Times*, April 10, 2013. https://www.latimes.com/entertainment/la-xpm-2013-apr-10-la-et-mg-lindsay-lohan-cries-letterman-20130410-story.html; Gay, Verne. "Lindsay Lohan and David Letterman: Well, How Did It Go?" *Newsday*, April 10, 2013. https://www.newsday.com/entertainment/tv/lindsay-lohan-and-david-letterman-well-how-did-it-go-v20678.

16 trey taylor. "This Lindsay Lohan Interview on David Letterman in 2013 Is Horrifying to Watch Now. Https://T.Co/LZxKVvbVB0." *Tweet @treytylor*, February 13, 2021. https://twitter.com/treytylor/status/1360661970924556291.

3

Just Real Bitches in a
Fake-Ass World

Britney's value as a pop star and cultural figure is no longer up for debate. She had a smash hit four-year Vegas retrospective and had been given enough "legacy" and "icon" awards from the VMAs and Teen Choice Awards to fill a jacuzzi. Even her most everyday outfits have stuck in the cultural imagination: the pageboy cap and the T-shirt that says "dump him"; the all-denim dress; the shaved head and black FILA sweatshirt. Critics, who were lukewarm about Britney through most of her career, now regularly cite *Blackout* as evidence of Britney's innovative approach to Top 40. *Blackout*, with its forward-looking production and self-aware commentary about fame, has come to stand in for Britney's newly recognized importance as a musician, not just as a cultural figure.

But in 2007, the mainstream media was ready to treat Britney as a has-been. Three days before *Blackout*'s release, *MTV* published a short piece called "Britney Spears' Fans

... Who Exactly Are They?" It seemed that Britney's former prime demographic—tween girls—was notably absent from her fanbase. Ruben Garay, the founder of Britney fan site *World of Britney*, told the publication that she had managed to "piss off every single mom in America with her antics . . . So do you think that mothers . . . want to take their kids to a Britney Spears concert? No, forget it."[1]

Garay had a bone to pick with Britney. In December of 2006, ten months before *Blackout* debuted, he quit running *World of Britney* (*WOB*). The site had been around for six years, and in that time it transformed from a standard-fare DIY fan site into a behemoth. Garay doesn't quite fit the mold of your typical Britney fan. He's a straight man who started the site because he thought Britney was hot. Garay created a simple Britney news blog that compiled and presented updates about the star aggregated from across the internet. But even in its early days, *WOB* had big aspirations: it planned to launch a "fan section" with fan-written poems, fan art, anecdotes about meeting the Pop Princess, and "Emily's Corner," a news and opinions section written by a thirteen-year-old girl. Over time, the site would put in these features and more; *WOB* became a veritable production company, creating music video edits, sketches, podcasts, and documentaries about Britney in-house. Its motto: "Living up to each fan's expectations 24/7." But after a while, Garay felt alienated from Britney. He couldn't reconcile her increasingly erratic, even violent, behavior with the sweet teen pop idol he once loved. He explained, "I think that *World of Britney* has had its run . . . its feet are not holding firm anymore, not because of my ability to run it, but because I believe Britney is, unfortunately, done."[2]

Though *MTV News* seemed pessimistic about Britney's ability to retain her star power, it seemed that people were listening to Britney after all—they just wouldn't admit it. "Gimme More," *Blackout*'s first single, was a certified hit. When the article came out, the song had sat firmly in the *Billboard* Hot 100 for more than a month, becoming her then highest charting hit since her debut single, ". . .Baby One More Time."

Garay had a hypothesis as to who exactly was still fawning over Britney. Britney still had fans, he said. He told *MTV* that Britney's biggest fans could be split into two demographics: "the gay community" and "the fans that are just as much a train wreck as she is."[3] (*TMZ* confirmed this theory, reporting that "Gimme More" was a hit on the gay club circuit. West Hollywood clubs like Fubar, Here Lounge, and Eleven told the tabloid that "Gimme More" was one of their most requested songs.) Ruben's tone suggests he characterized the Britney fan base as the "gay community" and the "trainwrecks" to undermine the legitimacy of her stardom, as if to say she'd lost her grip on the mainstream. To him and to *MTV*, this was almost the same as having no fans at all. *MTV* didn't get any quotes from this apparently core demographic.

Yes, Ruben may have intended to insult her fan base. But we can read this characterization more generously. Though she may not have been as ubiquitous as she once was, Britney attracted a much more devoted audience who identified with her struggles as well as her successes. These fans, predominantly gay men, found something to love about the dark, unpredictable Britney on *Blackout*.

Sure, when *Blackout* came out, the mainstream media wasn't prepared to take it seriously. To her detractors, Britney seemed like a superficial party girl too unhinged to sing. But these fans used their growing collective power on still-nascent internet forums to defend Britney as a person and as an artist. Fans picked apart *Blackout* on Britney forums from the privacy of their computers, keeping Britney relevant and critically interesting even when publications declared her downfall. When the mainstream had abandoned her, these fans finished the project that Danja, Bloodshy, and Avant began on *Blackout*, reframing Britney's chaotic public persona and casting it as a form of art, a fiction that could protect her against the cruel machinations of the music industry and celebrity culture. These fans would have answered *MTV's* question ("Britney's fans ... who exactly are they?") if anyone had bothered to ask.

Fandom has always been seen as a deviant form of intimacy: it's unconditional love without the expectation of reciprocity, love so unrequited it becomes absurd. Some skeptics treat fans as the ultimate consumers, willing to gulp down any product a record label will spoon down their throats. Others think fans are cult members, a violent mob willing to do anything for their favorite star. Many dismiss fan behavior as if it were a mental illness, never hesitating to point out that "fan" is believed to be an abbreviated form of the word "fanatic."

But as the internet spread and got more robust, fandom became less and less of a marker of strangeness. Social media has narrowed the gap between ordinary people and the celebrities they admire. The intimacy between fan and celebrity now seems more reciprocal, as cadres of fans create fan edits, memes, and trends for others to participate in, which in turn allows them to interact directly with the celebrities they love, getting their quips retweeted and questions answered. It's not uncommon for a celebrity to pluck a comment from obscurity and respond to it directly in a public forum, for all to see.

These days, fans on the internet straddle a line between toiling in obscurity and becoming public enough to affect the trajectory of the star herself. Stan accounts on Twitter garner follower counts large enough to make them micro celebrities. Being a fan could even be, for a lucky few, a path to fame and fortune, as in the case of Lil Nas X, who leveraged a Nicki Minaj stan account with followers in the six figures into a pop career of his own. Rather than passive consumption or violent hysteria, fandom can be seen as a form of cultural production like art, criticism, or journalism. Even academics and critics often feel the need to identify themselves as "fans" of what they write about as a way of signaling that they're experts in the subject but not hoity-toity elitists looking down on the plebs from above.

Fandom has transformed from a marker of deviance into a source of cultural capital. Pop stans are some of the biggest contributors to contemporary culture. They've popularized the slang we use, the memes we send back and forth, the music that gets played on the radio. On the modern internet, pop success is not (only) about the number of plays a song gets, but the depth of fans' devotion. These days, there's no queen of pop. It's a feudal system, in which armies of stans command remarkable power over record and tour sales. It no longer pays to be likable and middle-of-the-road—pop stars court fans by being dark, raw, and weird, in both their sound and their public persona.

But it's still a mystery how exactly we got here. The early days of internet-fan culture are poorly documented. Sites like *Pulse Music*, or pop-specific chats on AOL, where users debated about their faves are now gone. The ecosystem of fan sites and Myspace pages where fans amassed enough power to begin to affect culture writ large have almost completely disappeared.

Fandom in the *Blackout* era helps provide answers. It was a hinge between the fan culture of the early internet and the stans we know today. For the first time, the internet had diminished the inherent power imbalance between a fan and a star so much that a fan could use the depth of their devotion to distinguish themselves from other faces in a crowd. Fandom, which once seemed deviant, juvenile, and foolish, could now be seen as rational: the fan supports the star, and in return gets a full-time job, one that could earn money and admiration and even minor fame.

One of the fans that pioneered this trajectory is Jordan Miller, the founder of the most popular Britney forum after the rise of social media, "Exhale," a subset of his larger media empire called *BreatheHeavy*. If you spend any time in the Britney fan world, Jordan's hard to avoid. He has a YouTube channel; he appears in Britney documentaries. Even today, if you read a couple of posts on "Exhale," a notification will pop up. "Hey friend, Jordan here. ☺" it says, attached to a selfie of Jordan, naturally lit, with his blonde hair slicked back. "I noticed you've been lurking on *BreatheHeavy*'s Exhale forum as a guest. I would love it if you'd take a moment and register an account."

He started the site in 2004. Back then, the online Britney community was almost entirely anonymous. Still, the people I interviewed who participated in online Britney fandom in the early days suggested that it was "a lot LGBTQ+ people." While Britney's appeal to teen girls was obvious and well documented, early Britney would have been a strange choice as a gay icon. In the early days she seemed like a sweet, ambitious girl trying to have it all. She was normal, even bland. Unlike old-school gay icons like Judy Garland or Joan Crawford, Britney was put-together, and uncontroversial. One Britney fan told the *Guardian*: "For my generation of gay men of a certain age . . . she was probably Baby's First Diva. Her first album dropped when I was in fifth grade, and was 'safe' for my parents to let me listen to."[4]

Jordan, when he first joined the Britney online fan community, was still deeply in the closet. His username, which he used to comment on various Britney forums, was "gymnastdude182." "Gymnast dude" after his preferred after-school activity, and "182" after pop-punk band Blink-182, which he had no particular affection for but thought would make him seem straight. Jordan related to Britney's confidence, in both her free-spirit sexuality and her can-do attitude. Whatever she did, she succeeded at: she sang, she danced, she sold. Like Britney, Jordan was a competitive gymnast throughout his childhood and adolescence. Six days a week he went to gymnastics practice for hours at a time, doing backflips as his coach, a former Olympic champion for the USSR in 1992, corrected his form. Every day he shuttled between school, home, and the gym. Britney was a reprieve from the businesslike aspects of his daily life.

As he spent more and more time on Britney forums, Jordan found that there was an intensity to the Britney fan world that excited him. Like gymnastics, or even the pop charts, the Britney fan world was ruthlessly competitive, with its own set of rules. Fan communities traded in scoops, in exclusive information. The best sites published unseen photos, fun facts, even where Britney was hanging out any particular night. There was a hierarchy of Britney sites: the best blogs published the biggest scoops before everyone else, had the closest relationships to Britney and her posse, and garnered the most traffic. In this context, *World of Britney*'s motto—"meeting each fan's expectations 24/7"—wasn't just a promise; it was a flex. The high-octane, fast-paced nature of the fan world excited Jordan so much that he considered starting a fan site of his own. "I was like, I'm going to be number one," he told me. The thought of being on top nagged at him: "I kept thinking that I will do whatever it takes to be the most-trafficked, number-one Britney website." Though he joined the Britney fan community out of a desire to connect with others about a favorite star, his own desire for recognition prompted him to start a fan site. Besides, the two goals didn't seem mutually exclusive.

Before he could begin constructing a website of his own, he had to learn how to mock-up layouts in Photoshop, code, and select eye-catching stories for his home page. He reached out to the moderators of his favorite fan sites for advice, but they were reluctant to reveal their secrets to a potential competitor. But Jordan was also a fifteen-year-old kid with a dogged desire to learn. How dangerous could he really be? After inhaling any information he could find on web design, Jordan was ready to launch his site; all he needed was a name. On a trip back from a gymnastic competition, he had his headphones in on the bus, listening to a remix that Pharrell made of "I'm a Slave 4 U." The bridge samples the sound of Britney panting. Jordan bought the domain "breatheheavy. com" in 2003, and it has been his ever since.

Like most fan blog owners, he wanted to focus on Britney's music, sharing unreleased demos or spreading rumors about who she was working with on her next album. In June 2003, when Jordan started the site, she was about to begin her tour for *In the Zone,* but seventy-two hours after the site went live, she broke her knee during a rehearsal, he told me. She quit the tour, and wouldn't release a full-length album for the next three years. As Britney stopped working, bloggers had to focus on her personal life—they had no other option. Jordan tried to keep things light and positive. When Britney was ranked the most annoying star of 2004, he wrote "If no one cared about you, no one would write about you . . . well, I think it's a compliment."[5] But as the news got more and more negative, so did the content of his blog. He couldn't ignore the bad news. He had to break stories to get on top, no matter what they were. So Jordan, a teenager, found himself competing with the tabloids.

After a day of school, he would have thirty minutes before gymnastics practice started to go home, change, and with any spare minutes he had, update *BreatheHeavy*. After gymnastics, he would go home and update the site again, and compulsively check the internet to see what Britney news was out there until he fell asleep. His site's catchphrase was: "updated 7 to 10 times a day," courting the most rabid fans. His doggedness paid off; after stumbling on some Britney news, he'd report it immediately. Though other outlets would publish the full story a few hours later, Jordan did it first, and for those brief hours, *he* was the primary source of Britney information. After this happened over and over again, his audience came to rely on *BreatheHeavy* to keep them in the know. *BreatheHeavy* was where the true fans could congregate and consume Britney content before everyone else.

As the wins piled up, the traffic got more and more addictive. This only compounded once *World of Britney* shut down, and *BreatheHeavy* could finally take its spot in first place. As his site blew up, Jordan became acquainted with people on the inside of Britney's world, who could give him anonymous tips to keep him ahead of the news cycle. Still, at times he'd be so desperate for a scoop that he'd receive a tip and look the other way, even if the details didn't add up.

I mentioned to him that in some ways, his fan site didn't seem so different from the gossip blogs he reviled. After all, blogs like Perez Hilton's were also scrappy upstarts vying with the bigwigs for exclusives. When I said this, Jordan winced. He wasn't a *tabloid*, he explained. He emphasized that the site's tone was positive, always rooting for Britney even in her darkest moments. He saw *BreatheHeavy* as a safe space where Britney could go and read supportive comments from people who loved her, if she felt so inclined. But he intimated that sometimes, he felt less sure that his site was an uncomplicated force for good. His perspective was more sympathetic, sure, but he was still reproducing the many scandals that plagued her. Jordan couldn't control the comments, and in the site's early days, he didn't moderate. *BreatheHeavy* was open for people to express their views anonymously, making many conversations on the site toxic as well as supportive. Though in 2006, he was more successful than ever, there were times where it seemed that his site was gaining traffic at Britney's expense.

In 2007, Jordan hoped that the conversation might return to Britney's music after three long years of posting gossip. He stumbled on some footage of Britney in her black Mercedes convertible, pulling out of Shutters, a luxury hotel on the Santa Monica beach, with a shadowy, hard-to-see figure in the passenger's seat. The paparazzi cameras accost her, but Britney ignores them, staring ahead blankly, hiding her face behind her giant sunglasses. She turns on the stereo and plays her own demos, a series of ballads: "Baby Boy," a wonky lullaby, "State of Grace," a wistful love song, and the much-awaited "Rebellion," another attempt at a kiss-off track about the celebrity machine in the vein of "Mona Lisa." She didn't seem to care about playing these demos ahead of her label's release schedule, or breaking her non-disclosure agreement (NDA). It seemed that Britney was ready to release new music, on her own terms. It was only a matter of time.

In the ensuing months, Jordan got his hands on a series of demos of Britney's newest album, which didn't yet have a name. The track list included the demos she played for the paparazzi, along with a few other songs, many of which made their way onto the final album—he remembered listening to "Cold as Fire," which would end up on *Blackout* as "Hot as

Ice." Jordan had gained enough power that he could override an entire label's worth of executives and release *Blackout* himself, if he wanted. Jordan's fandom didn't brand him as a freak or a pariah, but instead, a winner, not just in the insular community of online Britney fans, but in the wider world.

Ultimately, as *Blackout*'s release date approached in fall of 2007, Jordan decided not to leak the album. He eagerly anticipated Britney's return performance at the VMAs, a venue she had dominated. But Britney gave the worst performance of her life. She took the stage at the VMAs to perform "Gimme More," but wobbled through her dance moves rather than performing them full-out. Clearly lip-syncing, she seemed lost onstage, her eyes unfocused and her movements imprecise. Such a sexless, lethargic performance was unimaginable six years prior. Who could forget when Britney peeled off a blazer on the VMA stage to reveal a sheer, sparkled catsuit, or when she sashayed with a pale-yellow anaconda wrapped around her shoulders?

Critics, tabloids and viewers alike tore her apart. Perez Hilton told *Reuters*: "Everybody knows Britney lip-syncs, but that's because she dances so much. She barely danced in this. It was painful. It was embarrassing. And I loved it!"[6] There was no end to what she did wrong: her lingerie was ugly, her stomach too bloated, her dance moves unprofessional. This was supposed to be her comeback performance, her first time onstage in three years, and she botched it.

Though Jordan didn't leak *Blackout*, someone else did, so Jive released the album a few weeks early so as not to compromise too many sales. Even with a new release date, *Blackout*'s performance disappointed. All of Britney's previous albums debuted at number one, but *Blackout* missed the mark. Previous Billboard rules prevented albums sold at only one retail outlet from entering the charts, to prevent large companies from artificially inflating sales numbers, and *Blackout* debuted the same week as the Eagles's *Long Road out of Eden*, sold exclusively at Wal-Mart. The difference in sales between the two albums was stark: the Eagles sold 711,000 records, over twice Britney's 290,000 sales. Though some Britney fans and studio execs worried about a conspiracy on Wal-Mart's part of doctoring the numbers, *Billboard* couldn't find any evidence. So *Billboard* altered the rules that very week, putting the Eagles on top. The Eagles beat out Britney based on a technicality, but even excluding *Billboard*'s arcane rules, there's no denying that Britney's sales were meager compared with the first-week sales of her previous albums: *In the Zone* (609,000), *Britney* (746,000), *Oops!... I Did It Again* (1,319,000). To be fair to Britney, when you start your career with a platinum-single and yearly chart-topping albums, there's nowhere to go but down. But if her critics were looking for a narrative of failure, this was it.

Even Jordan suffered after the VMAs. Britney's team had allegedly invited Jordan to party with Britney in Vegas the day before her comeback performance. He posted a photo of himself with Britney on *BreatheHeavy*'s forum, "Exhale," but users didn't treat it kindly. One Britney fan I spoke with, Gabriel, said that though he was part of "Exhale" for a while, the environment got too combative after Jordan met Britney. Another fan, Luis, put it much more bluntly: "He faked this picture with Britney . . . it was clearly Photoshop." Though this inter-fan squabble seemed relatively minor, for

Luis, it indicated larger problems with Jordan's approach to fandom. "Jordan was the first fan that sold out," he told me. Luis alleged that Britney's manager at the time, Sam Lutfi, had been giving Jordan exclusive information, and Luis was suspicious about how uncritically Jordan reproduced Sam's version of the events. "Britney was being held hostage. Sam used to take her phones," he said, "but this photo proves 'Oh, Britney's out and about,'" making Sam seem like a benevolent influence, even though Britney was suffering behind the scenes. "When you become the center for information [about Britney] what narrative are you pushing about her?" he said, "[Jordan's] rise was tied to Britney's downfall."

The *Blackout* era made Jordan an influencer, someone that could meaningfully affect Britney's trajectory and the cultural conversation around her. But *Blackout* also created the opportunity for another fan to swoop in and steal his spot as Britney's number-one fan: the newly ascendent Cara Cunningham.

Cara Cunningham was a YouTuber and already a bit of a celebrity, albeit only on the internet, at a time when online popularity didn't translate into corporate sponsorships and raucous tours and an inevitable pivot to pop stardom. Cara had a popular Myspace video channel. In her videos, she performed under the pseudonym "Chris Crocker." She mixed muscle shirts and eyeliner, spoke in a light southern accent, and showed off her scrawny frame. Her first hit was "Bitch Please," a one-minute clip where she repeated the phrase in various tones. Then her most popular video became, "This and That," a motivational speech, where "You bitches wanna fight me? Girl, you bitches wanna fight me?" she shouted directly to the camera, scrunching up the sleeves of her crop top to reveal her skinny biceps. After two months on YouTube, it had been viewed 300,000 times.

After Britney's VMA nightmare, Cara put up a video that would soon become more famous than the performance itself. She sat in front of a loosely strung-up sheet, with peroxide blonde hair and running mascara. It seemed like she had already been weeping for a while. Cara cried: "Leave Britney alone! You're lucky she even performed for you bastards. She's a human being!"[7] Then she paused to wipe her eyes with the back of her hand.

The video generated more views than any viral video had before, to the tune of 43 million hits by 2012, two million of which appeared in the first twenty-four hours that the video was up. Almost immediately, "Leave Britney Alone" propelled Cara into the mainstream, getting her interviews on CNN, Fox News, MSNBC, The Today Show, Maury, and more.

People wondered what to make of her. Her YouTube name was a pseudonym, and though Cara frequently railed against her bible-belt hometown, she never revealed its location, preferring to say she lived on "Real Bitch Island." Eli Sanders summed up the confusion in a profile of Cara for Seattle alt-weekly the *Stranger:* "I'd guessed [Cara] was an art student, young looking but not actually that young, who was lying about [her] age [stated as nineteen] and living somewhere in Manhattan . . . The gays I know who have never lived in a small, conservative town (people like myself) thought [Cara] must be an ironic urban art-fag with something to say about the absurdity of fagginess and race relations. Those who have lived in rural America pegged [her] immediately as a type they know well, or once were themselves—the seething gay kid, trapped in a place that can't tolerate homosexuality and punishes flamboyance."[8] In other words, was she really who she said she was? Or was her over-the-top flamboyance an act?

It turned out that Cara Cunningham did live in the rural south, in Bristol, Tennessee. Unlike the still-closeted Jordan, Cara had come out in seventh grade. Bullied and harassed in high school, Cunningham left to be homeschooled, and lived in almost complete isolation, aside from her immediate family. The claustrophobia and bigotry of her hometown felt more and more crushing. She turned to the internet to escape.

Cara initially started phoning what she called "black gay tranny phone hotlines" to find other queer people to talk to. Cara told *Edge Media Network,* "I had a lot of free time and no friends, so I started studying their behavior. And I was like, 'What is this lingo that I've never heard?' It's like so exciting. It was a whole new world that wasn't accessible to me." [9]Inspired by the "energy" of the people she talked to on the phone lines, Cara appropriated a sassy, bitchy persona as an outlet to express her queerness, when she couldn't do so offline. Her YouTube persona was flamboyant and confident, like on "This and That" where she told her "haters" "you ain't saying shit to me, girl." Later, she said, "I don't even know if that was me."[10]

Cara had been a Britney fan her whole life. She wallpapered her bedroom with images of the starlet, slept on a Britney pillow, kept the time on a Britney clock. In one grainy clip, she's watching a DVD of Britney onstage. "I can transform into Britney Spears. You didn't know that?" She whispers to the camera, punctuating the phrase with a laugh. "I get to watch it, and then with both of my eyes I examine Britney, and I become her . . . I'm planning to kind of steal her. Then I'm going to be her."[11]

In a way, she did. There is an eerie similarity to Cara's and Britney's stories. Both were from the deep south, both were criticized for their looks, with sloppy eyeliner and fake blonde hair, both were ruthlessly torn apart for their failures to adhere to gendered norms: Cara for being too femme, Britney for not being feminine enough. Britney's amateurism onstage knocked her out of the A-list, whereas Cara's bravura performance brought her to a similar cultural ubiquity to the Princess of Pop.

Though they both succeeded in the wake of life in the *Blackout* era, Cara seemed to be Jordan's complete opposite. Unlike Jordan, who diligently catalogued Britney's successes behind the scenes, Cara was melodramatic, femme, clearly queer, and flourishing in front of the camera. Cara's form of fandom was simultaneously more obvious and more opaque than Jordan's. It was clear how she felt about Britney, but less clear what these feelings *did*. Jordan and Cara seemed to map two paths forward for fans on the internet. Jordan used the internet to shroud his identity and practice a form of fandom that could be considered respectful and reciprocal. Meanwhile, Cara emphasized herself above all else, alongside the ridiculous, non-normative aspects of fan culture. She leaned into the stereotype of the hysteric fan in a way that didn't seem to benefit Britney at all.

At the time, Britney fans like Jordan thought Cara gave them a bad name. If this video, like the rest of Cara's output, was a shtick, it could function as cultural commentary or satire—Cara's over-the-top delivery could read as a mockery of the melodrama and vacuousness of fandom, or even of Britney herself. But if she were serious, she'd be another tragic diva like Britney: poorly made-up, histrionic, out-of-control. To Jordan, Cara seemed to be mocking Britney and her fans by exaggerating their most grotesque qualities, and using Britney's abjection to advance her own career.

But Cara didn't seem to be mimicking Britney. She spoke about her in the third person, and didn't emulate any of her qualities other than, perhaps, her blondness. She wasn't playing a "Britney Fan" either. Though her dramatic performance of screaming and weeping could be associated with the worst stereotype of hysteric teen-super fans, nothing indicated she was playing a type.

Cara had performed versions of this character before: over-the-top, bitchy, blonde. But Cara's persona on "Leave Britney Alone" is more emotionally vulnerable, and more explicitly feminine; weeping with running black mascara running down her face is the stereotypical image of a woman in pain. Around the time of the video, Cara's mother had just returned from a tour in Iraq, and had developed an addiction to meth in addition to severe post-traumatic stress disorder (PTSD). The rest of the family disowned her, and she had no place to live. Meanwhile, Britney, another mother from the Bible Belt, flailed, struggling with addiction and retaining her connection to her children. "I've always looked up to Britney,"

Cunningham told *Rolling Stone*, "and the other woman in my life who I looked up to, my mom, was falling apart."[12] When she wept in "Leave Britney Alone," she wept for all the women in her life who were abandoned when they stopped doing everything right. "That moment was a slice of the real me," she said.[13]

The similarities between Britney and Cara also opened her up to criticism. Commentators and pundits piled on Cara just as they did on Britney. Most of the people who saw the video couldn't understand the mix of irony and sincerity in "Leave Britney Alone," especially since these viewers, for the most part, hadn't seen Cara's other content. "Leave Britney Alone" spread far beyond Cara's usual audience into the thunder dome of mass public opinion. The endless barrage of transphobic and homophobic comments pummeled Cara. "When I said ["leave Britney alone"] I had to fear for my life ... Physical attacks were made towards me at gay bars and out in the streets," she recalled, "This was during a pre-*Drag Race* time, before everyone and their mom was saying 'Yass queen!' It was a time of only embracing the heteronormative people in media."[14] She tried to use the momentum around "Leave Britney Alone" to her advantage, not unlike Jordan, perhaps as a way of launching a career in show business. But Hollywood didn't know what to do with a figure as iconoclastic and queer as Cara. She went out to Los Angeles and took a few meetings but nothing got off the ground. Cara had tried for so long to make it out of Tennessee, but after just a few months in Los Angeles, she was broke and tired and had to go back home.

In the *Blackout* era, Britney became more than just a celebrity. Through Britney, Cara could escape the constraints of her hometown and transform into a diva, exalted in her abjection. Meanwhile, Britney gave Jordan a way to be an ambitious professional. But only one of them was able to leverage the fruits of their fandom into a career. Jordan is now a certified Britney expert, appearing in articles and documentaries, and his recognition has only escalated over time, as the movement to end Britney's conservatorship, "#FreeBritney," became front-page news. Jordan is often credited with coining the hashtag "#FreeBritney," and as such, he has become a figurehead for the movement as a whole. As Luis put it to me, "Jordan became a spokesperson, but Cara became a joke, just like Britney."

Though in the present, Jordan seems content to have his career tied to Britney, Cara, rightfully, feels spurned. She was pummeled for sticking up for Britney, even though she was right—we should have left Britney alone. At the time, no one seemed to acknowledge "Leave Britney Alone" as an act of bravery and deep empathy, not even Britney herself. According to the tabloids, she found Cara "creepy," and thought that "Leave Britney Alone" was "insulting" and "difficult to watch." Cara's Britney fandom brought her into the public eye, but also eclipsed all other aspects of her identity and subjected her to unending barrages of homophobic and transphobic abuse. Cara had even been rejected by other Britney fans. She showed up at *Blackout*'s pre-CD sale at the Virgin Megastore on Hollywood Boulevard. "I'm excited because it lets all the Britney fans come together and have a Britney moment, and we just get to join hands and share our love of Britney" she said.[15] But she never got to experience that moment of camaraderie. As she approached in a tight blue dress and a blonde bob, everyone standing in line booed. "You're a gross whore," yelled one. "Kiss my ass, because I got to do a *contribution* to Britney, fuck you," she responded. "It turns out Britney fans are some of my biggest haters," she said, after the incident.[16]

Eventually, she renounced Britney altogether. In one clip, she stands in front of a blank wall, warning her audience: "I will no longer respond to 'Britney Boy.'" In another, we see her tear down every single poster of her in her room. As crumpled pictures of Britney's face fall to the floor like dry leaves, Cara sobs, repeating, "She never even thanked me."

Over a decade later, as Britney's conservatorship case picked up public support, Cara posted to her social media accounts a reflection on her time being Britney's number one fan. "Me saying 'leave Britney alone' was never really the issue," she wrote, "Michael Moore said it and no one batted an eyelash. The reason no one took me [seriously] was because I was a gender-bending teenager and the reaction to me was transphobic."[17] It wasn't just straight society that spurned her. She said, "This hate was also directed towards me by other LGBT people . . . who were embarrassed of me because of the way the media made fun of me. Which made them feel I gave them a bad name."[18] Later, she told *NPR*: "I think no one now can argue with what I said—they just didn't like the messenger."[19]

But ultimately, Britney benefited more from the sympathy of a "gender-bending teenager" than from more normative "messengers." Cara's performance in "Leave Britney Alone" reframed Britney's messy "trainwreck" persona just like

Blackout did. *Blackout* served a similar role for Britney that YouTube served for Cara; it allowed her to escape the brutalization of her daily life and inhabit a world where she was in control. Britney's aggressive, boldly sexual persona on *Blackout* mirrored Cara's. Britney flips off the haters with "It's Britney, Bitch," Cara with "Bitch, Please." The questions of authenticity surrounding "Leave Britney Alone" mirrored those surrounding *Blackout*. Critics fretted over whether songs like "Piece of Me" or "Gimme More" reflected Britney's true feelings, while viewers had a hard time reconciling Cara's earnest sadness with her camp sensibility. These personas, straddling the line between sincerity and theatricality, were direct reactions to the societal forces that constrained their behavior. "Leave Britney Alone" showed that the once untouchable Britney had been brought down to earth, allowing fans like Cara to identify with her in a way they never could've before.

Britney's messy, confident *Blackout* persona appealed to other young queer fans, too. One fan told me that the song "Gimme More" "made him gay." He couldn't quite articulate why—Britney is about as straight as they come (save, perhaps, for her infamous kiss with Madonna onstage at the VMAs), and *Blackout* has no explicitly queer themes. But the confidence that Britney displays on *Blackout* helped Britney's younger queer fans have sympathy for the parts of themselves that didn't fit normative boxes. Luis echoed this notion: "*Blackout* was the sexual awakening for a lot of us," he told me. "This is when [gay men of my generation] started having sex. And having sex as a gay person is confusing. It's incredibly terrifying. Growing up gay when we did, we really were shamed for our sexuality in the same way that Britney was. And then to get this very dark, sexual and sort of adult album … It was like a permission to embrace our sexuality, to actually try the thing you fantasize about."

For most of her early career, Britney was a model of success in white womanhood, performing femininity so perfectly and dutifully that she could amass power in a system primed to exploit her. When the system turned on her, record execs and critics expected that she would try and regain her status by appealing to normative taste. Instead, she gave us *Blackout*, an album in which she embraced her subversive qualities. The criticisms leveled at Britney—that she was too passive, too feminine, emotional, chaotic, and violent—were strikingly similar to those leveled at her queer fans, many of whom were still coming to terms with their identities in a hostile, discriminatory world. In a total subversion of her original teen-pop persona, *Blackout* aligned her with the most marginalized.

Britney rebuked normative standards of success, and fans like Cara Cunningham loved her for it. Cara went on Maury, looked into the camera, and told the world, "Before I'm an American, I'm a Britney fan." This statement proved controversial. In the context of the Iraq war, Cara's refusal to be patriotic, among her other controversies, frightened the networks that were in talks of picking up her reality show. She lost the deal, her only prospect for a career in show business. But why should she be patriotic? Poor and femme and stuck in rural Tennessee, Cara was never a candidate for the American dream. Her mom went to Iraq a patriot and returned homeless and traumatized. America had failed them both; it had failed Britney, too.

It was fans like Cara and Jordan that ultimately turned *Blackout* from a failure into a cult classic. While critics didn't see *Blackout* as Britney's story, many of her fans did. Fans paid attention to *Blackout*'s lyrics as evidence of her suffering. As Cara put it in "Leave Britney Alone": "Her song is called 'Give Me More' for a reason because all you people want is MORE! MORE, MORE, MORE, MORE!" Cara saw the irony in the response to her VMA performance. In "Gimme More" Britney railed against the the public's unrelenting cruelty, and in response, they just laid it on even thicker.

With this narrative in mind, the *New York Times* documentary *Framing Britney Spears* retold the story of her VMA performance more sympathetically. Backstage, Britney overheard comedian Sarah Silverman rehearsing jokes at her expense. "[She's] 25 years old and she's already accomplished everything she's going to accomplish in her life," Silverman said at the time, "It's mind blowing." These comments threw Britney off-balance. The pressure was too much. She felt that no matter what she did, people would always see her as a failure, so why try? She choked.

Silverman's jokes tore down Britney for her failure to adhere to the typical timeline of white-heteronormative adulthood. At twenty, she had achieved the American dream: she got rich, married, had kids, and rested on the laurels of her successful career in show business. Then she blew it all up. She no longer had a linear trajectory: she ended her marriage, lost custody of her children, stopped caring about her looks, didn't promote the album that could spark her comeback. Those who became even bigger fans after *Blackout*, Cara, Jordan, and the other "gays and train wrecks," understood this feeling. Britney's twenties fit Jack Halberstam's description of "queer time," in that its nonlinearity undermines the typical heteronormative path—career, marriage, kids, retirement—and its expectation of continuous personal growth. By relating to Britney's brokenness, her fans constructed a new narrative for her, one that rejects the normative trajectory of adulthood and celebrates her deviations from it. In one of her old YouTube videos, Cara infamously said: "I'm just a real bitch in a fake-ass world." On *Blackout*, so was Britney.

Cara and Jordan's generation and the generations that followed grew up on the internet, and for the most part would never know a life without being scrutinized by semi-strangers. Stans create fan edits, memes, and trends for other fans to participate in, which in turn allows them to interact directly with the celebrities they love, getting their memes retweeted and questions answered. They talk in Cunningham-like hyperbole, peppering their posts with appropriated slang. It turned out that *Blackout* soundtracked an Internet that didn't quite exist yet.

Britney herself was a burgeoning internet savant before her breakdown. She was one of the first celebrities to have a blog, which she called "Letters of Truth." It was a subsidiary of her personal website, and you could pay $25 a month to read what she posted. She began in 2004, after the release of *In the Zone*, documenting her aw-shucks family life, like Thanksgiving (she made "a roast with carrots, potatoes, corn and my favorite garlic bread"), and her love for her mom ("she always was and still is a Supermom"). Though this was her "official" fan site, it didn't seem like her management checked it or cared much about it, given how much of her blog Britney devoted to making fun of them. Britney's blog was a rare opportunity to see a version of Britney with her guard down.

Similarly, her reality show, *Chaotic*, pioneered the vlog format that would become so popular in the ensuing years. The show resembles a loosely structured YouTube video more than traditional reality TV; she filmed it all herself, occasionally flipping her digital camera around to get a selfie. There are no confessionals, nor are there scenes in a traditional sense. The show presents Britney going about her daily life, going onstage, certainly, but mostly goofing off. The best part of the show is seeing Britney blossom from behind the camera. Without explicit pressure to perform, her bubbly sweetness emerges. She does silly accents. We see warm camaraderie between her and her crew. She parties with them and asks them slumber-party questions from behind the camera, like "What's your favorite sex position?" Britney seemed interested in communicating with her fans more or less directly and cultivating an image that made her seem down-to-earth.

As things got progressively tougher for Britney, we stopped getting to see her life from her perspective. The show ended after just a season. By 2006, her mental health had tanked, and paparazzi tracked her every move. She no longer could control her own narrative. There were people everywhere, watching her every move. Some fans, like Ruben from *World of Britney*, could not reconcile this new narrative of Britney with her past self, while others, like Jordan and Cara, searched for new ways to tell Britney's story.

We still don't have an account of Britney's life from her own perspective. A few months after *Blackout*'s release, Britney was forced into a legal conservatorship, which placed all of her personal and financial decisions in the hands of her father. It seemed, at the time, that the conservatorship had helped Britney reach stability. She wasn't in the public eye quite so much, and she returned to recording and touring. It returned her to her nuclear family, who should have her best interests at heart. But immediately, fans saw this as a red flag. Jordan was one of them. "I always felt like this was wrong," he told me, but he emphasized that few felt the same way. "It was not a popular opinion back then to speak out against it. I got a lot of criticism about that. And I'm very grateful that I stuck to my guns." The quest to end Britney's conservatorship, #FreeBritney, has ballooned into an entire movement that includes lawyers, disability rights activists, reporters, and fans. They, like *Blackout*'s producers, her fans in 2008, and even me, are trying to tell Britney's story together when she can't.

We may not have to do this for long. On June 23, 2021, Britney addressed the court for the first time about her conservatorship. Before this, she hadn't been able to speak freely, without her father, her lawyer, or her "team" cutting her off. For twenty-four uninterrupted minutes, she told the story of her last thirteen years since *Blackout*'s release. Speaking at a breakneck pace, she listed an endless barrage of abuses, from the law and her own family. She spoke about being forced to take lithium, a drug that made her "[feel] drunk" and "mentally impaired." She had been imprisoned in a rehabilitation facility, where nurses and psychiatrists watched her morning, noon, and night. She was given an intrauterine device (IUD) against her will, to prevent her from having any more children. She felt so abused by her court-appointed therapist that she got on her knees and "thanked God" when he died.

Near the end of her speech, she mentioned that she no longer wanted to keep her life secret, and that she wanted to continue to tell her story in her own words. "For my sanity, I need the judge to approve me to do an interview where I can be heard on what they did to me," she said. "Actually, I don't want an interview—I'd much rather just have an open call to you for the press to hear ... I need that to get it off my heart."[20] A few months later, Britney announced that she would be writing a memoir, published by Simon and Schuster, dangling the potential of a coherent account of her life from her own perspective. But unlike in 2008, publications like MTV don't have to wonder who would listen to Britney speak her mind. We're right here.

Notes

1 Kaufman, Gil. "Britney Spears' Fans: As Blackout's Release Looms, Who Exactly Are They?" *MTV News*. October 22, 2007. http://www.mtv.com/news/1572480/britney-spears-fans-as-blackouts-release-looms-who-exactly-are-they/.

2 Dresdale, Andrea. "Britney's Top Fan Web Site to Close." *ABC News*, December 29, 2006. https://abcnews.go.com/Entertainm ent/story?id=2757547.

3 Kaufman, "Britney Spears' Fans."

4 Goldstein, Nancy. "Why Is Britney Spears so Appealing to Gay Fans?" *The Guardian*, December 12, 2013, sec. Opinion. https://www.theguardian.com/commentisfree/2013/dec/12/brit ney-jean-spears-new-album-gay-fans.

5 Miller, Jordan. "National Enquirer—December 28." *BreatheHeavy.Com* (blog), December 30, 2004. https://web.arch ive.org/web/20041230135942/http://www.breatheheavy.com/ home.php.

6 Goodman, Dean. "Britney Spears Earns Scorn for MTV Performance." *Reuters*, September 10, 2007, sec. Internet News. https://cn.reuters.com/article/us-mtv-idUSN063990492 0070910.

7 *2007: Leave Britney Alone! - CNN Video*. https://www.cnn. com/videos/bestoftv/2012/01/06/sot-news-to-me-leave-brit ney-alone-chris-crocker.youtube.

8 Sanders, Eli. "Escape from Real Bitch Island." *The Stranger*, May 31, 2007. https://www.thestranger.com/seattle/esc ape-from-real-bitch-island/Content?oid=232684.

9 Phillips, Tony. "Chris Crocker—'What's So Hard to Understand?'" *EDGE Media Network*, June 24, 2012. https:// www.edgemedianetwork.com/story.php?134490.

10 Ibid.

11 Veatch, Valerie, and Moukarbel, Chris. *Me @ The Zoo*. Documentary. *HBO Documentary Films*, 2012.

12 Volpe, Allie. "'Leave Britney Alone': Chris Crocker on YouTube Clip." *Rolling Stone*, September 13, 2017. https://www.rollingst

one.com/culture/culture-features/leave-britney-alone-chris-crocker-10-years-later-111918/.

13 Ibid.

14 Ilton, Josh. "Leave Britney Alone Video Led to Death Threats and Transphobic Hate for Chris Crocker." *Yahoo News*, February 12, 2021. https://uk.news.yahoo.com/leave-brit ney-alone-video-led-170106166.html.

15 Capelonga, Tom. "Chris Crocker's Reality TV Pilot Spotlights the Genesis of Internet Fame." *PAPER*, March 28, 2018. https:// www.papermag.com/chris-crocker-goes-to-hollywood-1-255 4109025.html.

16 Ibid.

17 O'Connor, Roisin. "Britney Spears Fan behind Viral Leave Britney Alone Video Speaks Out." *The Independent*, February 10, 2021. https://www.independent.co.uk/arts-entertainment/ music/news/leave-britney-alone-video-chris-crocker-b1800 229.html.

18 Ibid.

19 Pruitt-Young, Sharon. "Chris Crocker, 'Leave Britney Alone' Video Creator, Reflects On What's Changed." *NPR*, June 27, 2021, sec. Culture. https://www.npr.org/2021/06/27/1010355 669/chris-crocker-leave-britney-alone-video-creator-refle cts-on-whats-changed.

20 Aswad, Jem. "Britney Spears: Full Court Transcript against Conservatorship." *Variety*, June 23, 2021. https://variety. com/2021/music/news/britney-spears-full-statement-conserva torship-1235003940/.

Coda

Now that her conservatorship has ended, Britney finds herself at a crossroads, not unlike the moment of brief respite she wrote about on her blog in 2004. After so many years under the thumb of her father and the rest of her team, performing nonstop as part of her residency and ensuing tour, it's clear she wants to take a breather. She's engaged to her long-term boyfriend Sam Asghari, a model, actor, and personal trainer. She wants to have another kid. For now, she's enjoying the mundane freedoms that had been denied to her for the last thirteen years: driving to a restaurant, having a glass of champagne, splurging on a pair of sneakers.

Who knows when she'll return to music, or what it will sound like. A couple of years ago, Danja tweeted that he had been working on new tracks for Britney's tenth album. Fans wondered if he was making good on some offhand comments he had made at 2013's SESAC Pop Awards ceremony. A fan named Bradley Stern of *MuuMuse* approached Danja at the event and asked him if there'd be another *Blackout*. Danja responded, "I don't know when the next [*Blackout*] is going to be, but I believe there's going to be another one." A year earlier, Britney seemed to echo Danja's desire to make a sequel to *Blackout*. She tweeted on the fifth anniversary of *Blackout*'s release, "thank u all for loving the album as much as I do. *Blackout 2.0*?" In February 2022, she posted a video to Instagram of her dancing to "Get Naked (I've Got a Plan)," captioned "This is a tease 😊 of what's to come !!!!"

What would it mean to have a *Blackout 2.0*? The original *Blackout* was such a strange and unprecedented album that it completely changed the narrative of Britney's celebrity. *Blackout*'s producers emphasized the things that her critics dismissed her for—her voice's artificial qualities and the collaborative aspects of her process—reframing these supposed flaws as evidence of Britney's artistic prowess. *Blackout* let Britney rage against the celebrity machine that exploited her. Though tabloids dismissed her for being reckless, vapid, and slutty, *Blackout* made her unhinged behavior seem warranted as a response to the overwhelming surveillance she was subjected to.

Britney's confidence, dark sensibility, and self-awareness on *Blackout* attracted more vocal fans, who were for the most part, queer, and could see themselves in Britney. These fans fiercely defended *Blackout*, allowing it to be rediscovered in the 2010s as a cult classic. *Blackout* inadvertently set in motion an internet subculture-friendly model of speaking to few strongly, rather than as many as possible, a model that many new pop stars would imitate in the years following.

"In an oblique sense, *Blackout 2.0* has already arrived, with the explosion of PC Music and the first wave of the hyperpop movement, epitomized by A.G. Cook, Charli XCX, SOPHIE, Quay Dash, That Kid, Ayesha Electronica, Shygirl, Slayyyter, Kim Petras, and more. Many of these artists have cited Blackout-era-Britney as an influence, taking the record's uncanny, highly digital synth soundscapes and hyper-processed vocals to an even more exaggerated level.

Like Blackout, this movement celebrates the contradictions of pop music rather than attempting to resolve them. Projects like A.G. Cook, Hayden Dunham and SOPHIE's "Hey QT", and SOPHIE's *Oil of Every Pearl's Un-Insides* simultaneously revel in pop's euphoric heights while slyly criticizing how easily it can be canned, mocked and sold. Charli XCX's *Pop 2* spotlights her many collaborators, much like Blackout. PC Music and early hyperpop make the queer themes sublimated in Blackout explicit—Ayesha Erotica embodies the Y2K-era bimbo in its most transgressive form, and emphasizes that this persona is just as accessible to the "queens and the queers," the "girls and the gays," "the girls with big-ass lips … and the girls with big-ass dicks."

Like *Blackout*, these projects embrace pop stardom at its most maximal, incoherent, and artificial, along with all of its trappings: magazine covers photoshopped to perfection and washed-out paparazzi shots, flawless choreography and sloppy nights out, too-much makeup and uncanny-valley plastic surgery, uptalk and auto-tune, being down to fuck and look-but-don't-touch, bubbliness and cynicism, objectification and empowerment.

Britney Spears has always been synonymous with pop, its promises and its frustrations. Pop, like summer blockbusters and gas-station candy, exists to sell. The fickle whims of the public keep the genre from maintaining set aesthetic qualities: today's pop music could have dance instructions and rap features; yesterday's had dubstep drops and saxophone samples; tomorrow's could have pop-punk guitar solos or country mandolins with trap 808s. Any time you try to pin it down, pop swerves.

The best way to sell a pop star's new album is to dangle a new side of her in front of the public. Though we've seen her on magazine covers and red carpets, heard her while driving to work or wandering the aisles of the grocery store, we've never seen her like *this*. Pop is an industry built on longing— it sells concert tickets and moves records and can always be refueled with a new look, a new sound.

Since the early aughts, Britney has embodied this slippery, chameleonic quality. This made her captivating but eerie. There is something disquieting about a person who can inhabit so many contradictory identities. This inspired a never-ending hunger for the real Britney; tabloids, fans, and journalists alike wondered *Was she really a virgin? What medications does she take? What does her voice really sound like?*

Blackout takes the endless longing that fuels pop music and turns it on its head. *Blackout* presents a fun-house mirror full of Britneys, all as real as they are unreal. If this sounds scary or unpleasant, that's because it is. The public's fascination with Britney almost destroyed her. *Blackout* tells us that though we may long for the real Britney, we will never get it. But it also shows that we don't need the "real Britney"— we can revel in her many aliases, and celebrate them for the works of art they are. We can appreciate Britney the artist, while finally leaving Britney the person alone.

Near the end of the album's production, her team presented a music video concept for "Gimme More," *Blackout*'s first single. The original story involved a funeral, with Britney being kidnapped and then murdered.

But we can see drastic changes in the final product. The first shot shows a blonde, smiley Britney sitting at a bar. We hadn't seen this version of Britney for a while. This was the Britney that Jive Records fell in love with during the summer of 1997, wide-eyed and giggling in a knee-length dress. Watching this Britney is like watching a ghost. After a few shots of her laughing and drinking with her girlfriends, Britney notices a dancer about to take the stage. It's another Britney, wearing fishnets, a fedora, and a black wig. We see the scene from Blonde Britney's point of view, as Brunette Britney approaches a pole and begins to gyrate. Brunette Britney eye-fucks the camera and sings the song's opening line.

The rest of the video is lackluster. Britney's not a good pole dancer. She mostly flips her hair while bouncing around the stage. It ends with Blonde Britney clapping and smiling, the same as before, ignoring the fact that she has just been seduced from afar by her stripper doppelganger.

The image of Britney singing to her former self feels poignant. It mirrors the production, in which Britney's voice splinters apart. Some of her voices are high-pitched and coquettish, some deep and brooding, all equally artificial. Both Britney doppelgangers are costumes. The video ends, with its contradictions still unresolved, much like Britney herself.

Also available in the series